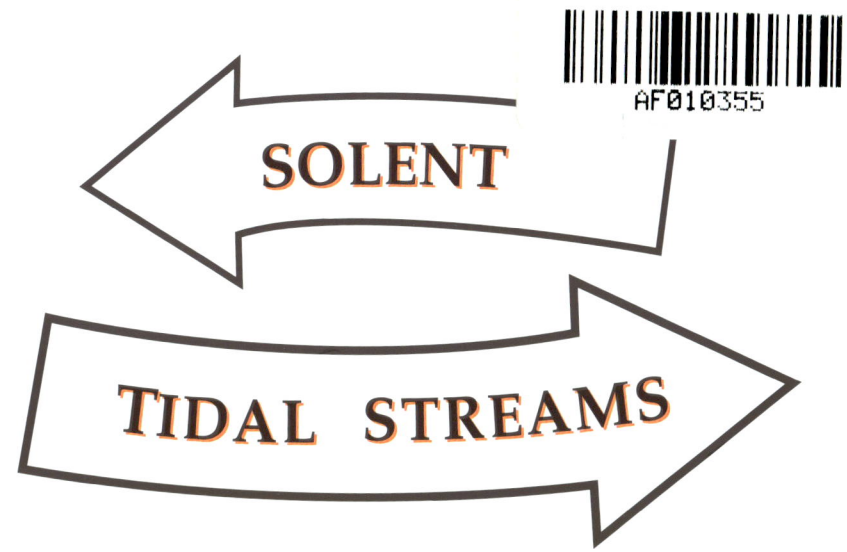

Peter Bruce

Contents

Solent Tidal Streams	2
Acknowledgements	7
Charts	8-33
Solent Area Distance Table	34
Other Peter Bruce books	35

Origins of the Solent

Eight thousand years ago the Solent did not have much tidal stream. From Bouldnor Cliff, two miles east of Yarmouth, what is now the Isle of Wight was joined by a forested neck of land to around Pitts Deep opposite, two miles east of Lymington. On the east side of this isthmus, a watercourse developed from Newtown, the Medina and Beaulieu rivers, the rivers that ran into Southampton Water and the rivers that ran out from Portsmouth, Langstone and Chichester. This combined flow formed into a south-going waterway that joined a major westerly-going river in the English Channel, a major component being the Seine, the channel of which is still discernible by Hurd Deep to the north west of the Channel Isles.

Earlier there was another more westerly connection of land which joined Hampshire to the Island between Sconce Point and The Needles. Consequently the Lymington River had to run out through the Yar valley to what is now the English Channel. Thus the long-accepted notion, first promoted 1862, that the Dorset Rivers Stour, Avon, Frome, and Piddle ran out through the Solent is now discredited. They ran out through gaps in the chalk ridge between the Needles and the Purbeck Hills where they joined up and flowed into the same major west-going river in the Channel.

With the passing of the last ice age, melting snow and ice raised the sea level some twelve metres, breaking through between the western fragment of the Island and the Hampshire shore, then finally breaching the neck of land between Bouldnor and Pitt's Deep, creating the Island of Wight and allowing a tidal stream to develop between the Island and Hampshire.

Solent Tidal Streams

Peter Bruce's original tidal streams books were derived from practical evaluation and local knowledge. Several well-informed people have given advice on their particular patch of the Solent, especially off Bembridge, Seaview, Cowes and between Fort Victoria and the Needles. More recently tidal model data from ABPmer (the research and consultancy group of Associated British Ports) has been used to improve previous editions. This information presents overall movement of the tidal streams, complementing isolated readings and provides more validity to interpolation.

Construction of the breakwater at Cowes in 2015 has altered the flow in Cowes harbour and, after the eastern channel was dredged to a depth of 2.25m in 2019; the tidal flow has noticeably increased on the south side of the breakwater, particularly on the ebb.

The High Water Stand

As both ends of the Solent are open to the sea, it is sometimes believed that this feature accounts for the double high water. However neither the Solent's double entrances nor the sun and moon alone can account for this quite rare phenomenon.

Advanced tidal theory explains both the double high water in the Solent and the contrasting double low water at Portland. At the time the tide is high at one end of the English Channel it is low at the other end and this induces a resonant effect, leading to the formation of harmonic waves. When the effects of the sun and moon and the harmonic waves are added together the result is a high water stand in the Solent and a low water stand at Portland. These characteristics would be present even if the Isle of Wight was not there as can be seen by the fact that a double high water also occurs at Christchurch, Poole and Swanage. All these harbours are in an area approximately half way along the 'tidal resonance chamber' of the English Channel. Both theory and practice indicate that the tidal stream rate in this area will be high and the tidal range low. However the consequence of the rotation of the earth, known as the Coriolis effect, also comes into play. Its result is to reduce the tidal range and the strength of the tidal streams on the north shore of the Channel and to increase the tidal range and the strength of the streams on its south side, hence the much greater tidal range on the French coast. We are lucky in the Solent to have a double high water which gives us a prolonged period when we can explore shallow creeks and have some hours to go alongside in places which dry out at low water.

Timing of Solent Streams

Elsewhere the change in direction of the tidal stream usually coincides with high and low water but this is not so in the Solent. The reason is the difference in the tidal range from one end of the Solent to the other. On a big springs there is 5m range at Portsmouth but only a 3m range at Lymington. As one might expect, the water wants to restore its equilibrium so, before high water has been reached, an ebb flow has already begun. This occurs first at the shallow edges of the Solent due to the greater momentum of the tidal stream in deep water. For example the stream will be seen to turn inshore at the mouth of the Lymington River 40 minutes before high water at Lymington Town Quay. Over the next 20 minutes the ebb tide will spread out to the middle of the Solent, turning last where the depth is greatest. Much the same effect occurs on the Island shore although the inshore ebb tide starts even earlier near Cowes.

An interesting variation in the main downtide flood flow of the Hurst Narrows constriction can sometimes be seen. Within the main body of the flowing water there can be significant changes to the rate of the stream, so instead of a uniform and homogenous flow, there are faster and slower streams within the main flow. Another feature of Hurst Narrows, again downtide on the flood, is the areas of swirling flat water amongst the general normal wave formation, caused by up-welling currents.

Reverse Eddies aka Counter Currents

Reverse eddies, or counter currents, are formed near the shoreline of a divergent area after a stream of sufficient velocity has passed through a restriction. In the west Solent, reverse eddies can be found either side of Sconce Point depending upon the direction of flow. After the flood has been running for an hour, a reverse eddy forms inside Black Rock, gradually extending out to the north of Black Rock buoy as the flooding tidal stream builds in strength. Likewise when the tide is ebbing a reverse eddy develops close inshore to the west of Sconce Point which then develops along the shore to Albert Ledge. In the Needles Channel, the close inshore current on the Island side precedes the change of direction of the main stream by about 1.5 hours, whether on the ebb or the flood. On the west side of Hurst Spit there are such strong eddies on a big spring tide that a counter- counter current, may be seen inside the main eddy. On the eastern side of Hurst beach, where there is a popular anchorage area, the stream is south going for most of the tidal stream cycle.

An extreme case of the complexity of Solent tidal streams can be illustrated by the following example. For a short time in the Hurst Narrows around High Water Portsmouth -1 hour (HWP -1) there are five areas of different tidal streams in close proximity. On the Island shore the tide is ebbing while in the middle of Hurst Narrows the last of the flood is still moving to the east. Then to the north of this there is an area of slack water before one reaches the ebb running at 2kn or so down the eastern side of Hurst beach and turning into the Needles channel. Finally the south-east going eddy will have just started on the SW shore of Hurst Spit running towards 'The Hurst Trap'. There are several other Solent 'traps' in addition to 'The Hurst Trap' which are described and clearly illustrated in *Solent Hazards & Secrets*. Such information is important to those who want to work against the slacker tides usually to be found on an inshore route. It is also valuable to know whether one is likely to encounter soft mud or hard rock in the event of grounding.

Perhaps the best known reverse eddy of all is off Cowes Green on the flood tide. Here the tide flows to the west for 9 hours out of the 12.4. Other west going eddies will be found off Norris Castle and in Stanswood Bay. East going eddies will be found in Gurnard Bay, Stokes Bay and off Seaview. Some of these eddies do not flow at neaps or are too close inshore to be of benefit to vessels without a very shallow draught but, even if the eddy is not running, the area where it can run will be where the contrary tide is weakest.

Shallow Water

The rate of the tidal stream over shallow patches, such as Ryde Middle and the Bramble Bank will speed up over the bank's leading edges and will be slower towards the downstream end.

Effect of Barometric Pressure and Wind on Tidal Height

Marked variations in tidal height occur as a result of changes in barometric pressure. Local effects of wind can also affect the tidal height. For example in the Solent a high barometric pressure of 1040mb combined with a strong north or north east wind could lower the predicted height of tide by as much as a metre. On the other hand, storm surges with associated low barometric pressure, such as the one that occurred in the October 1987 'hurricane', can cause the predicted height of the Solent tide to be exceeded by a metre or more.

Effect of Wind and Barometric Pressure on Tidal Streams

Winds generate currents by themselves, and the stronger the wind the stronger the current. If the wind generated current is superimposed upon a tidal stream the net effect is additive, so the apparent time for the change in tidal direction may be advanced or retarded by the strength and direction of the wind. It is sometimes said that high pressure will delay the change in direction of the tidal stream at high and low water, whereas low pressure will bring the change forward, but there is no scientific evidence for this theory.

Effect of Rainfall

Another interesting phenomenon is the effect of heavy rainfall. In the river estuary of Southampton Water, a layer of fresh water, up to perhaps a metre in depth, forms above the salt water layer and continues to ebb long after the flood tide has started. This surface stream is coloured brown, tastes fresh and the flow is evident on buoys and posts. It can be misleading to the pilots of deep draught vessels, which are predominately influenced by the deeper tidal stream. The same effect may be experienced to a lesser extent in other Solent rivers. Away from river effects, the sub-surface tidal stream will follow the surface direction and will not vary more than about 20% from the surface rate.

Using these Tidal Stream Charts

Rates have been measured at mean high water spring tide which is when the Portsmouth tidal range is 4.1 metres. Apart from enhancing the rates and eddies compared with using a lower scale, it means that the rate shown may be halved to obtain neap rates, i.e. when the Portsmouth tidal range is two metres, the tidal streams run at half the rate of mean springs.

At the turn of a neap tide within the Solent, large areas of slack water develop that can last for two or three hours, particularly in the east Solent over Ryde Middle. Eddies do not develop at neaps to the same extent as at spring tides, and often not at all. On the other hand when the tidal range is greater than 4.1metres, the tidal stream rates will be larger than those shown, and eddies will be more pronounced. At the top of spring tides there is often no period of slack water at the turn of the tide, the stream merely becomes circular before the 180° change of direction.

The long finger of sand to the east of Ryde Sands, called the Debnigo, running out from Puckpool Point on the Island in the direction of No Mans Land Fort, significantly affects the tidal flow off Seaview. When the Debnigo is covered the tide tends to conform to that of the main stream, but once uncovered on the south going tide it causes an reverse eddy to form to its southeast.

The broad arrows shown on the tidal charts show the main streams and give an indication of where the tidal stream is strongest. At mean spring tide the average tidal stream rate should be that shown within the enclosed area of the arrow. Length of the arrow does not give indication of rate, merely direction and distance over which the adjoining tide rate numerals apply. Arrows pointing both ways on a single line indicate a stream that might be running either way. Slack water is shown as SLACK, or, when space is restricted, shown just as an 'S'.

Whilst tidal stream charts are of great help, especially when planning passages and when racing, navigators of the Solent should not forget that observation may be of equal value to predicted data. It often pays to observe a float or buoy to confirm that the tide is doing what it is expected to do. By this means it can be assessed whether the tidal stream is running on time, early or late.

Both Admiralty tide tables and Reeds almanac refer only to the first high water at Portsmouth.

Acknowledgements

I am grateful to ABPmer for providing computer model predictions of tidal current speed and direction throughout the Solent region. The data were used for wider context and generally bear a good resemblance to other existing data in the main channels. I am particularly grateful to Dr David Lambkin for his kind and erudite assistance.

I am grateful to the Cowes Harbour Commissioners, Captain Stuart McIntosh, the Cowes Harbourmaster and Dr Rob Nunny of Ambios for making available their latest tidal stream data.

The streams off the east side of the Isle of Wight are especially renowned for their capriciousness, so I am most grateful to Raymond Simonds, one of the most able helmsmen of the Sea View Yacht Club, for his advice and that of his friends and relations. Also thanks are due to an eminent member of the Bembridge sailing community who prefers to remain anonymous but who has gone to the trouble of coordinating local opinion to obtain better Bembridge tidal stream information for the book.

I am grateful to Commodore David Hughes RN, Major General Chris Elliott, Allan Collison Esq and Dr David Lambkin for proof reading the script. Also Tom Barnard Esq for using his graphic skills, especially to convert my amendments into user-friendly arrows.

Peter Bruce

July 2020

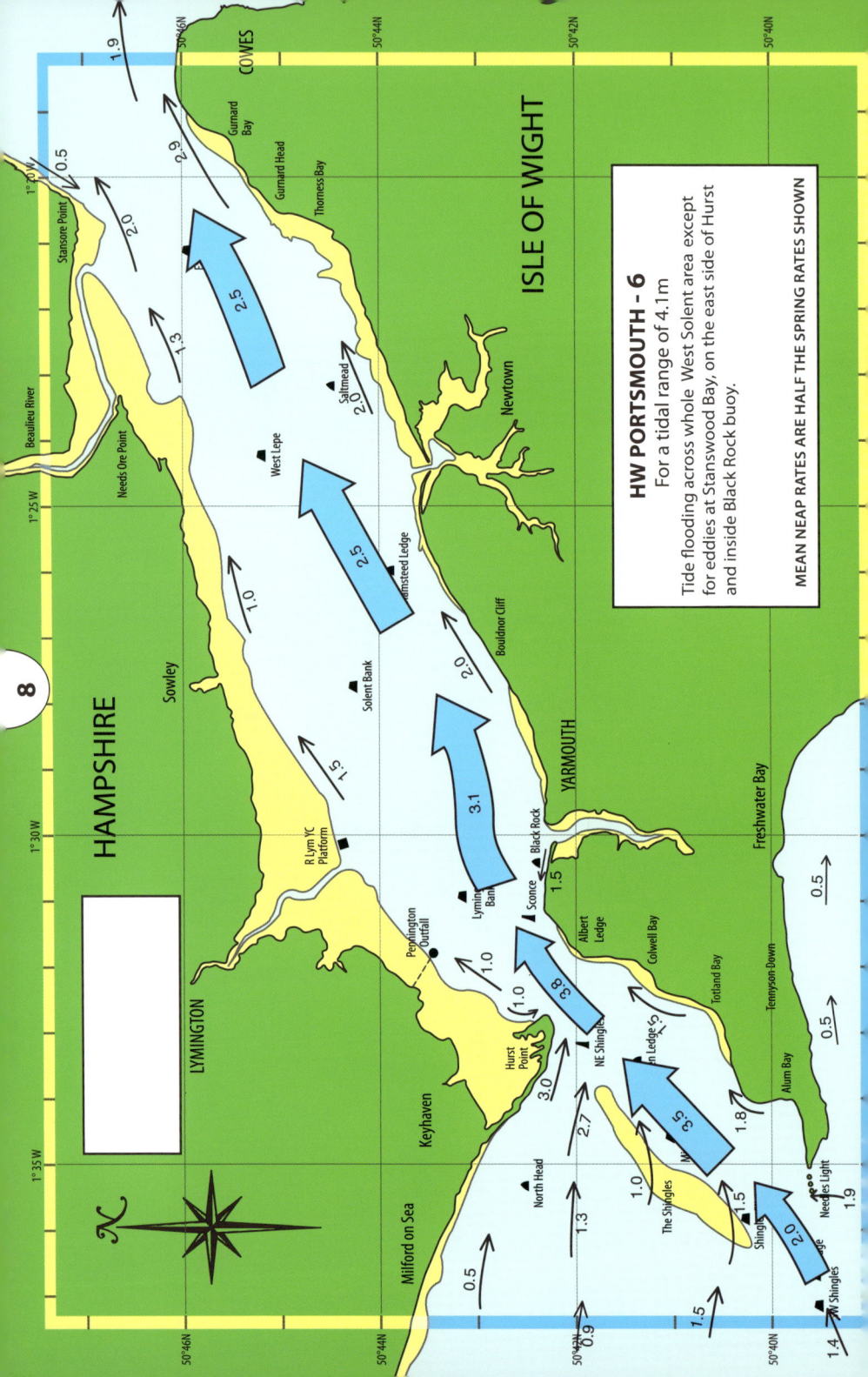

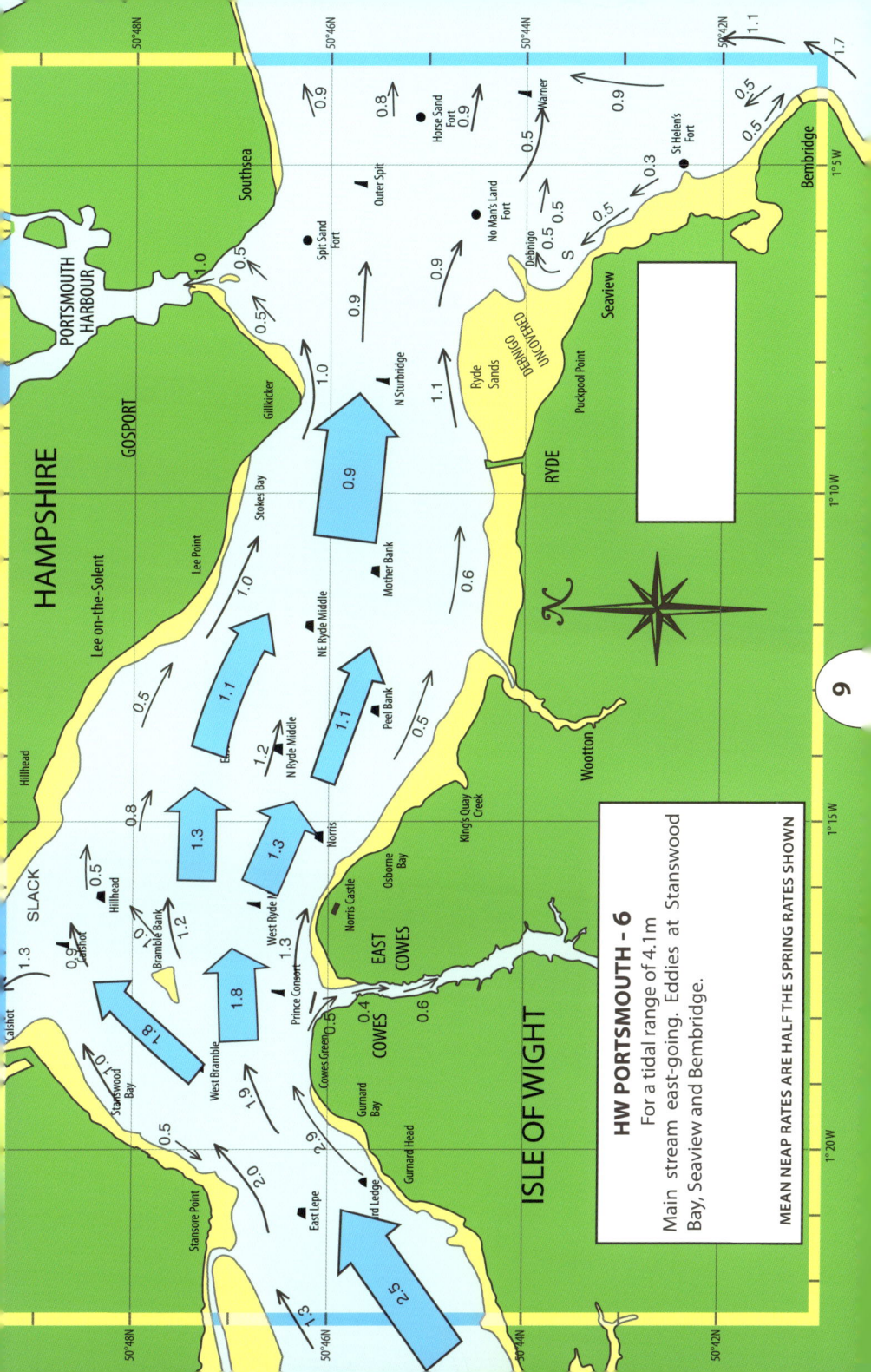

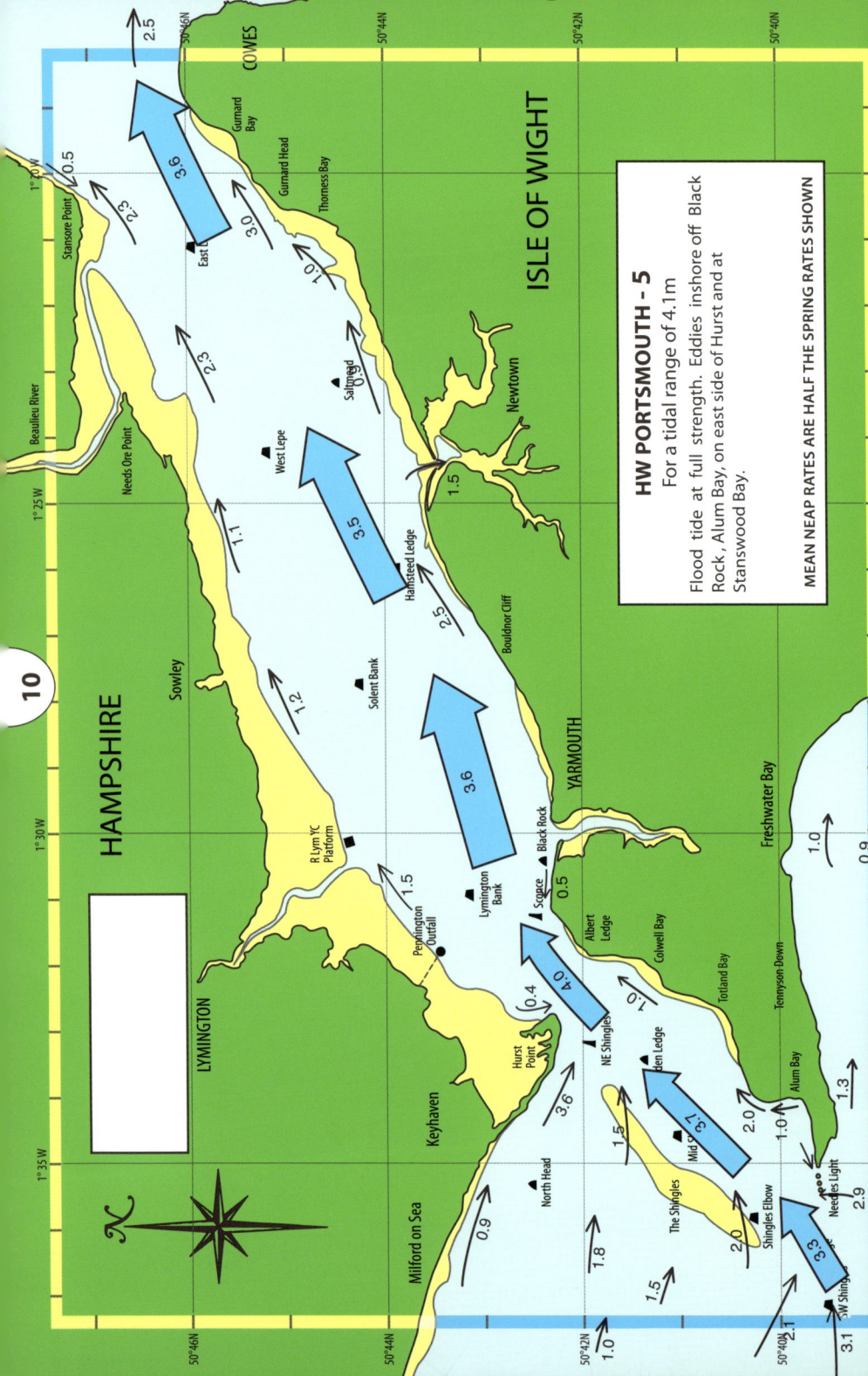

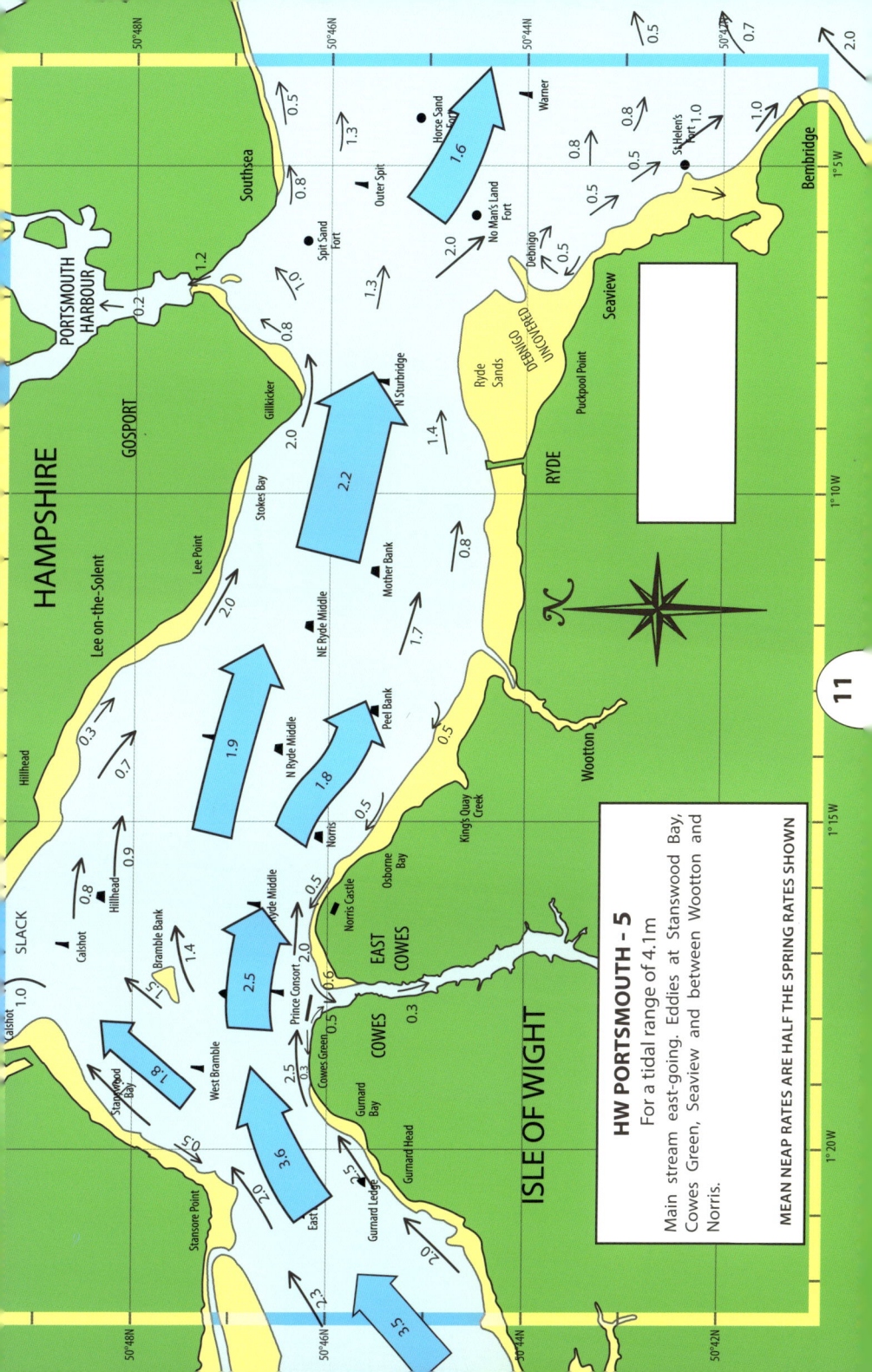

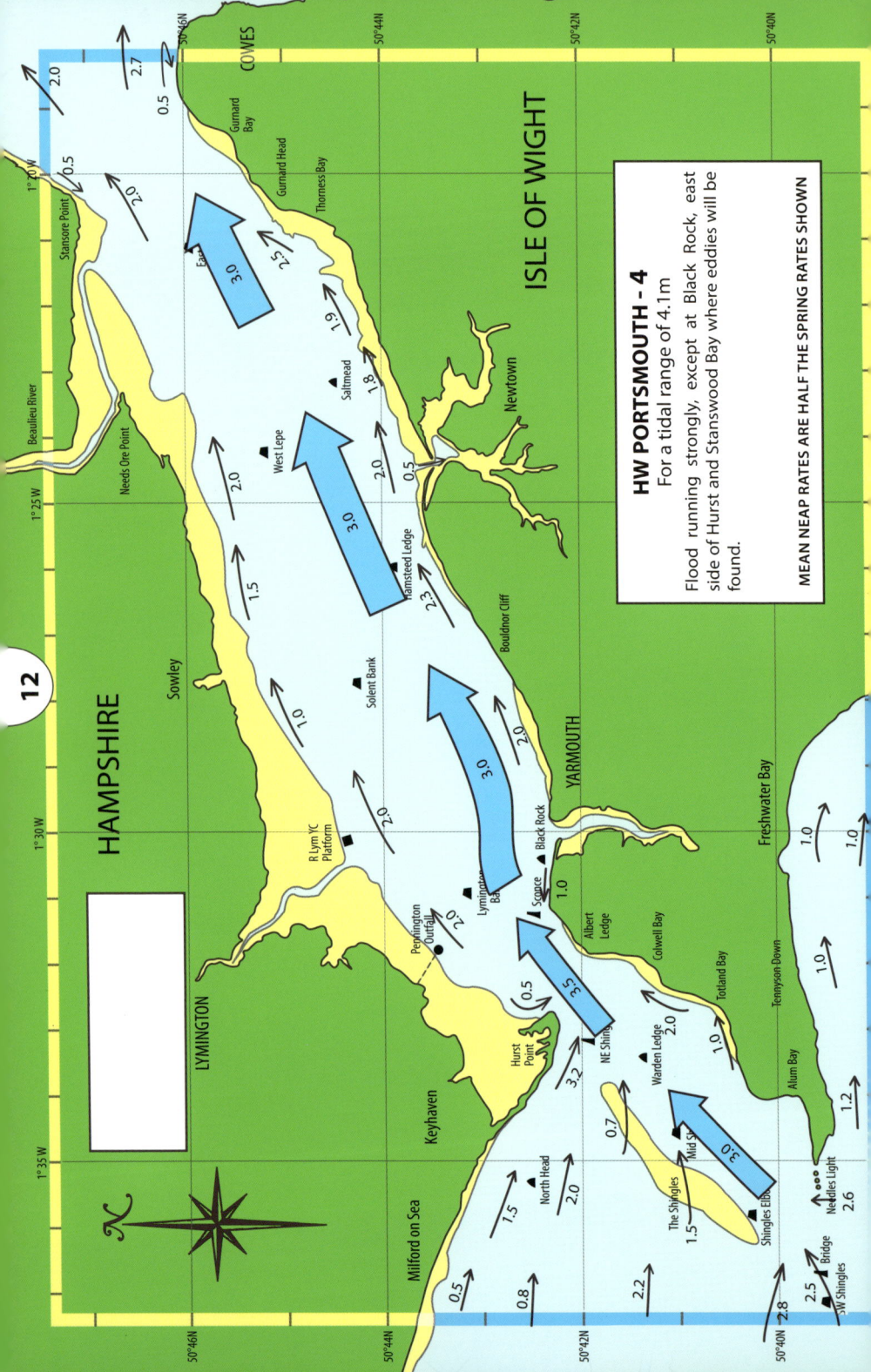

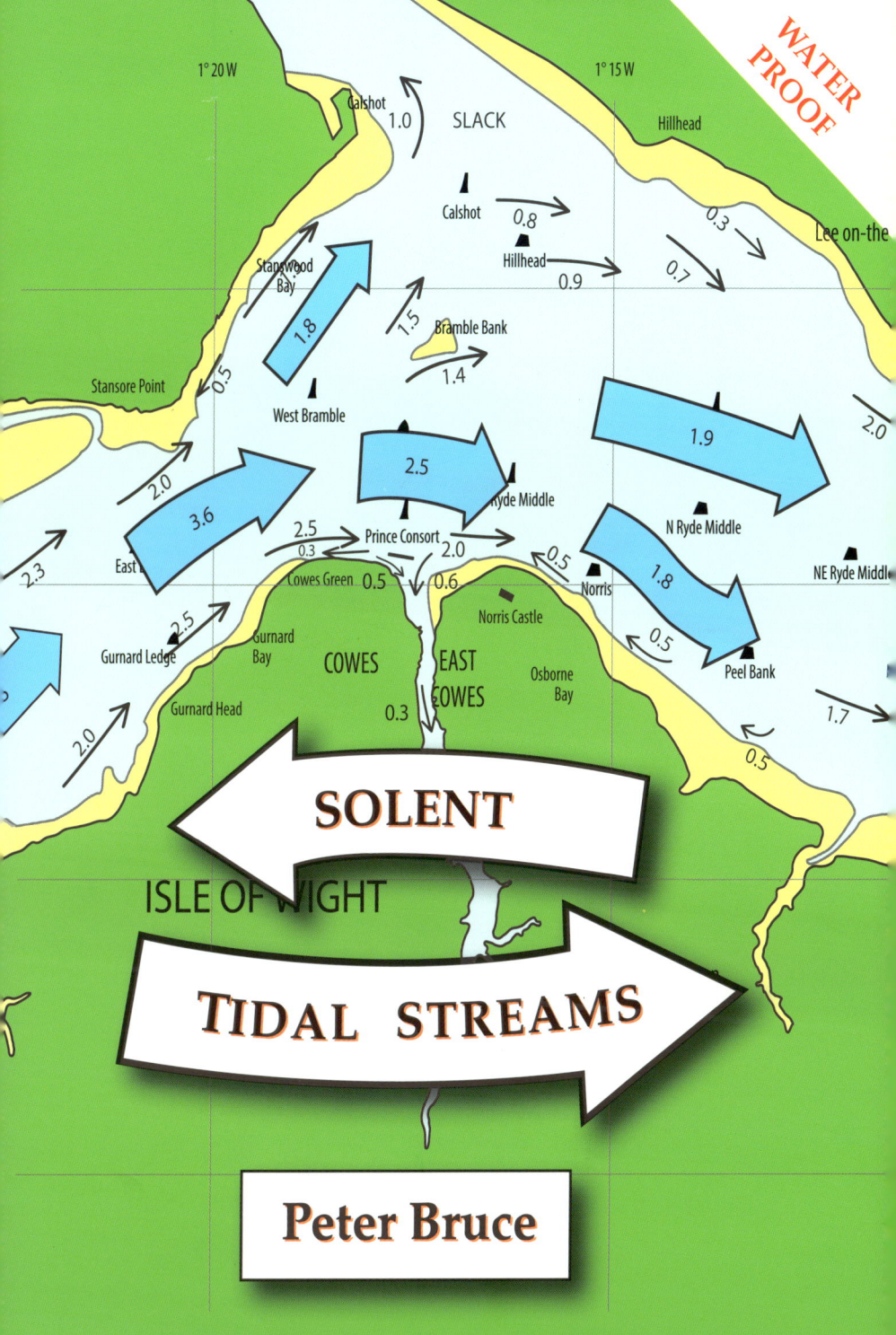

Solent Tidal Streams – Peter Bruce
First Edition Published July 2020

Other books by same author:
Solent Hazards
Wight Hazards
Inshore Along the Dorset Coast
Solent Tides
Solent & Island Tidal Streams
Tidal Streams between Portland Bill and St Albans Head
Heavy Weather Sailing

• • • • •

Copyright © Peter Bruce 2020
All rights reserved. No part of this book may be reproduced or transmitted, in any form or by any means, without the permission of the publisher.

• • • • •

Caution
Whilst every care has been taken in compiling this book, it is regretted that no responsibility can be taken by the author or publisher for inaccuracies or omissions, or for any accidents or mishaps resulting from its use.

• • • • •

Published by:
BOLDRE MARINE, Mayflower House, Lymington, Hampshire, SO41 3SN, UK
Tel: 01590 718912   E-mail: mail@peter-bruce.com   Web site: www.peter-bruce.com

Printed by:
CROSSPRINT, Newport Business Park, Barry Way, Newport, Isle of Wight PO30 5GY

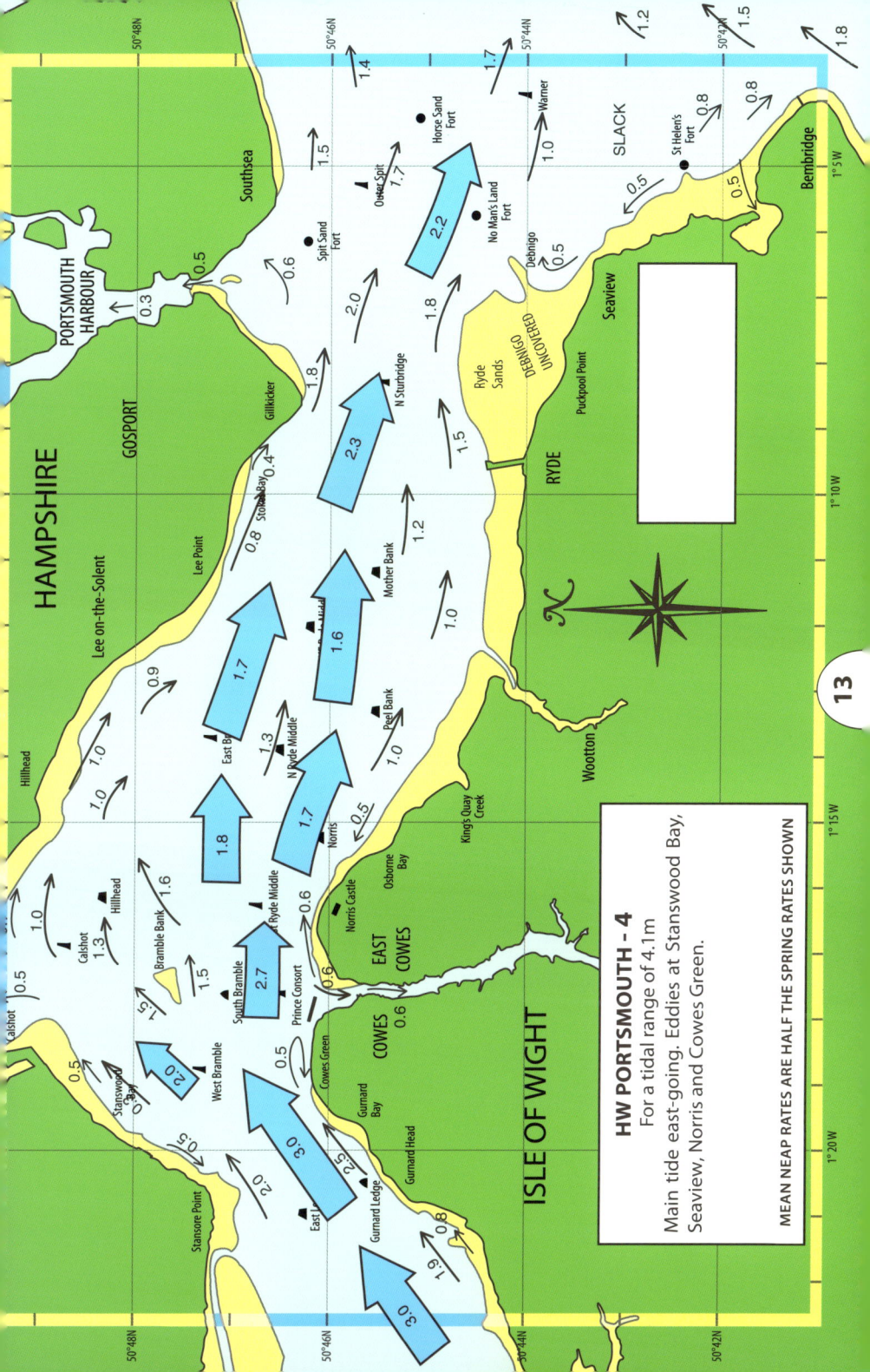

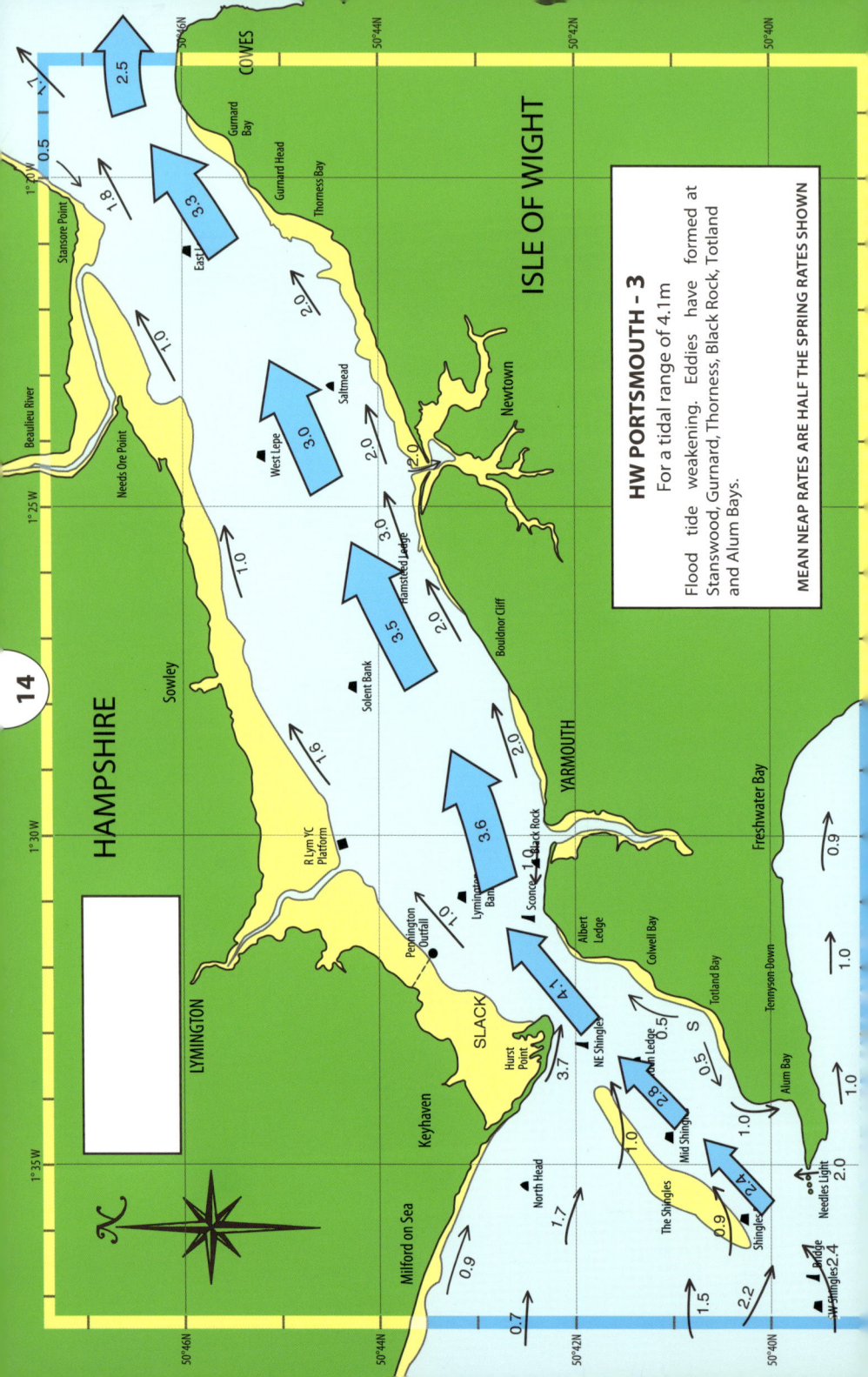

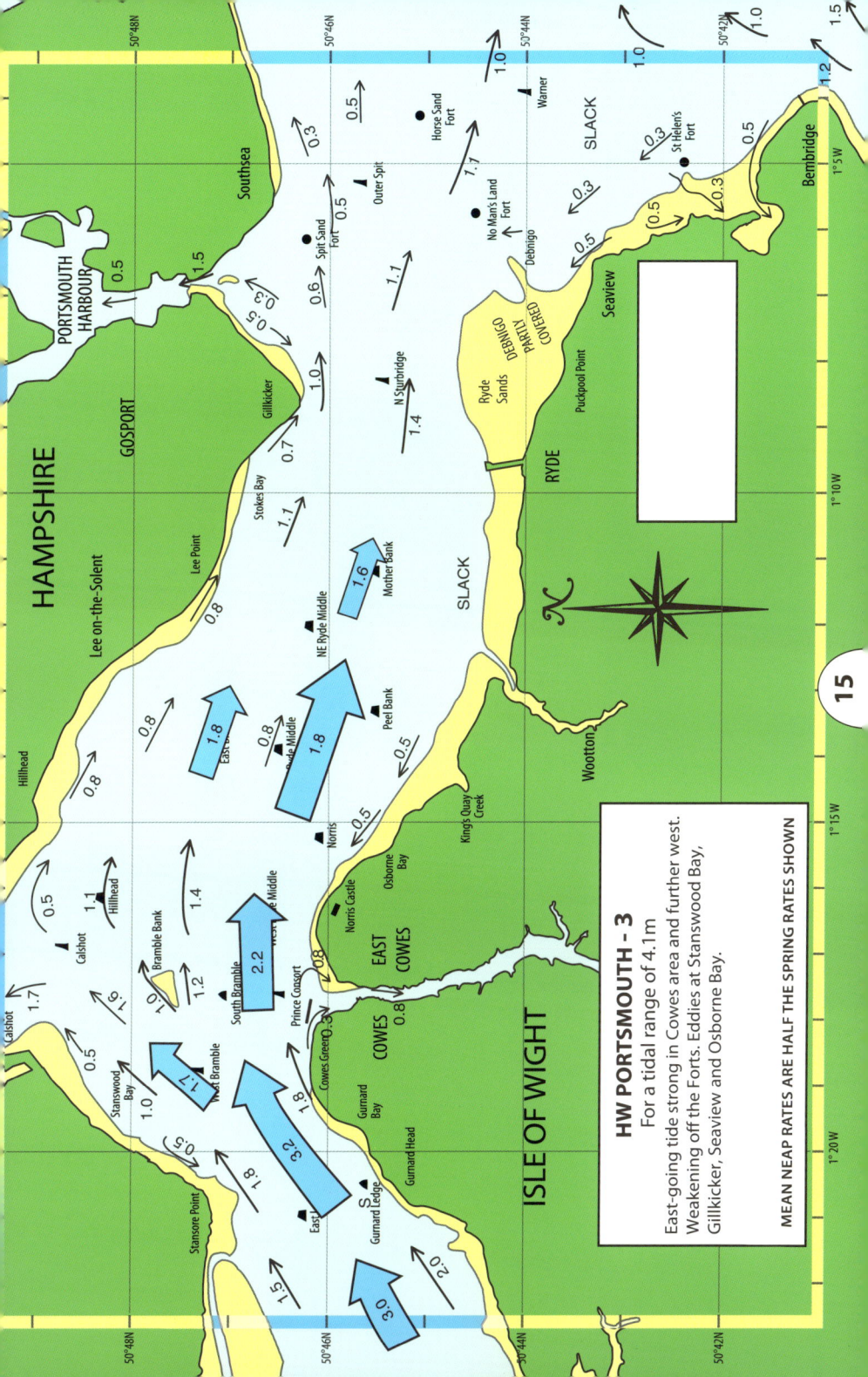

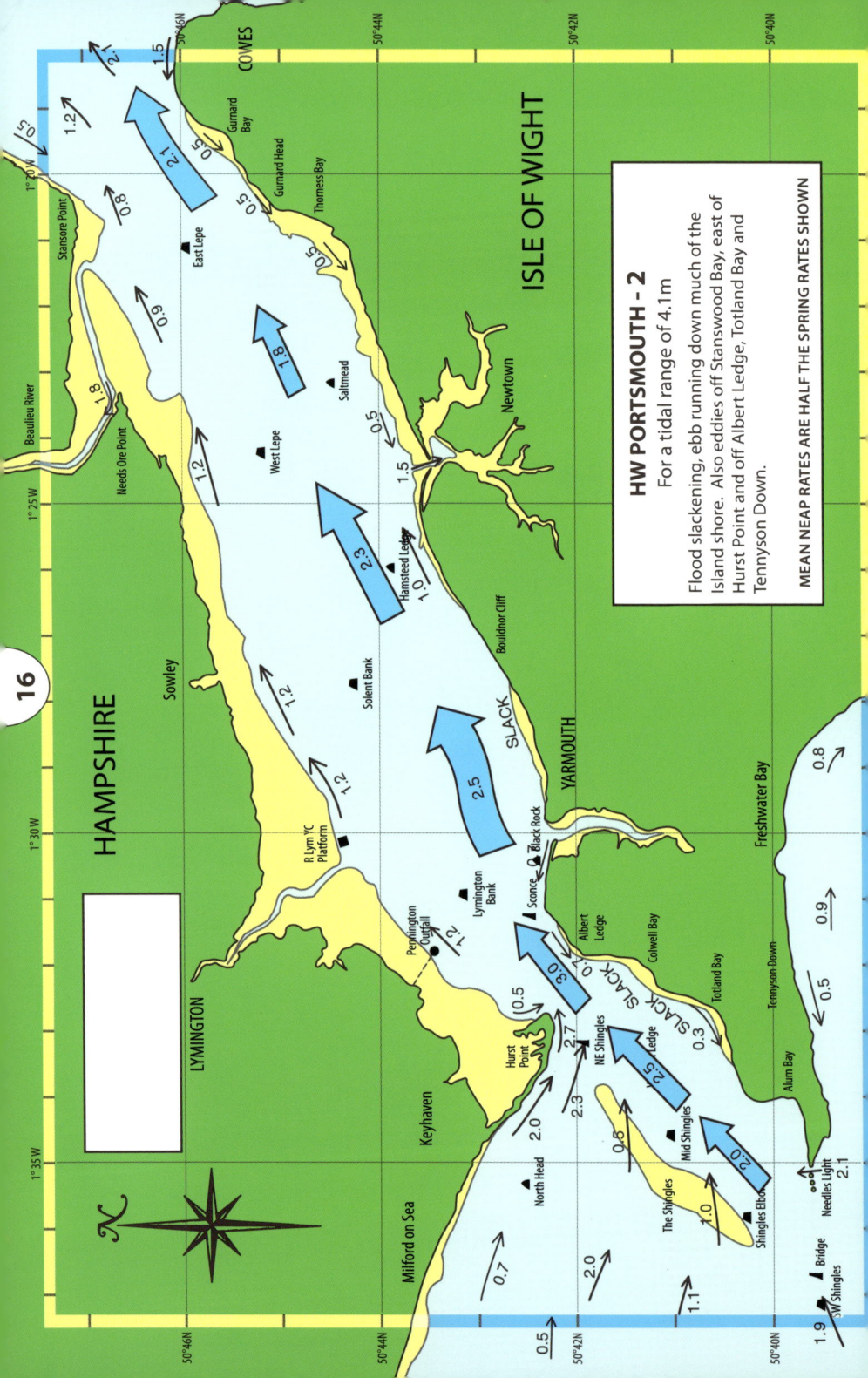

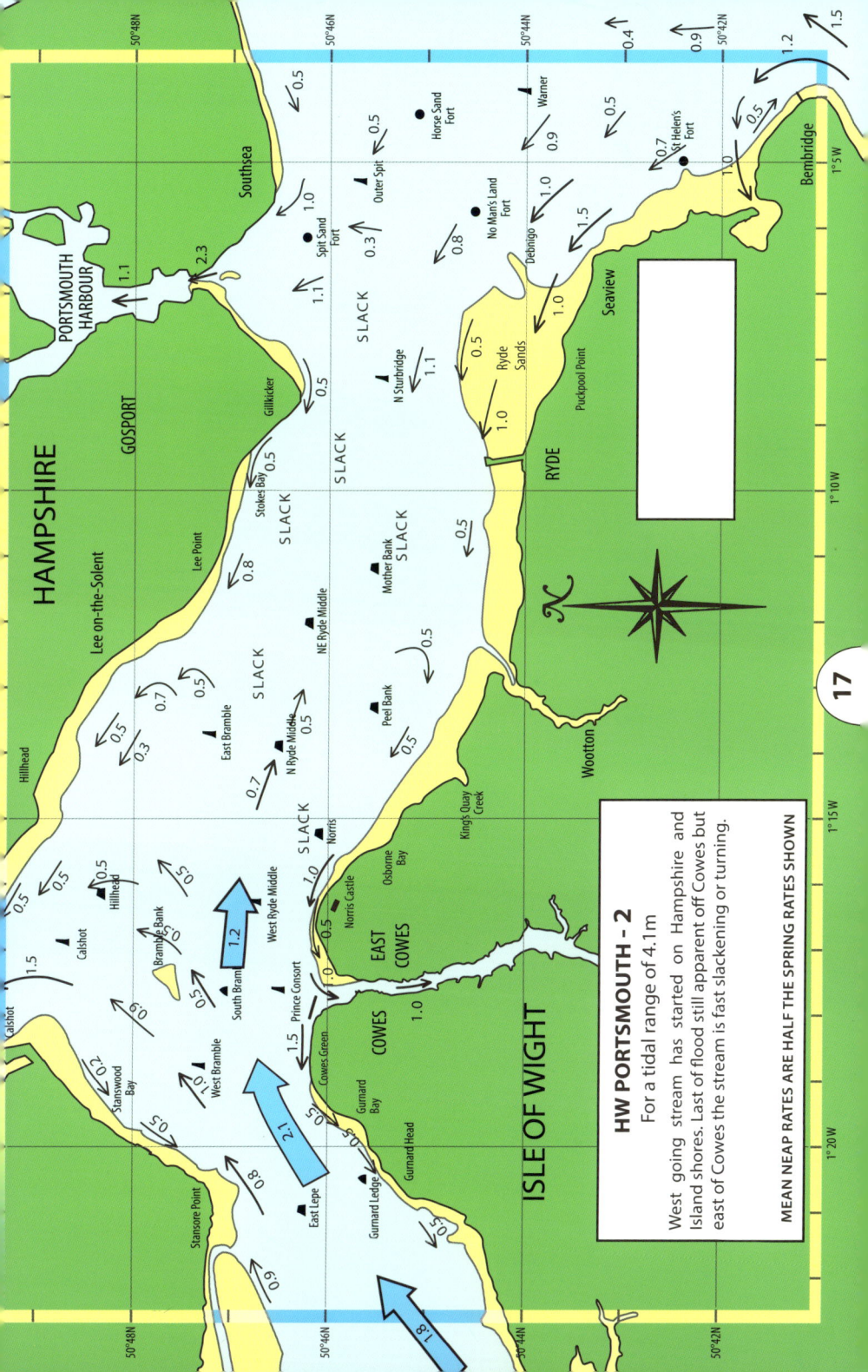

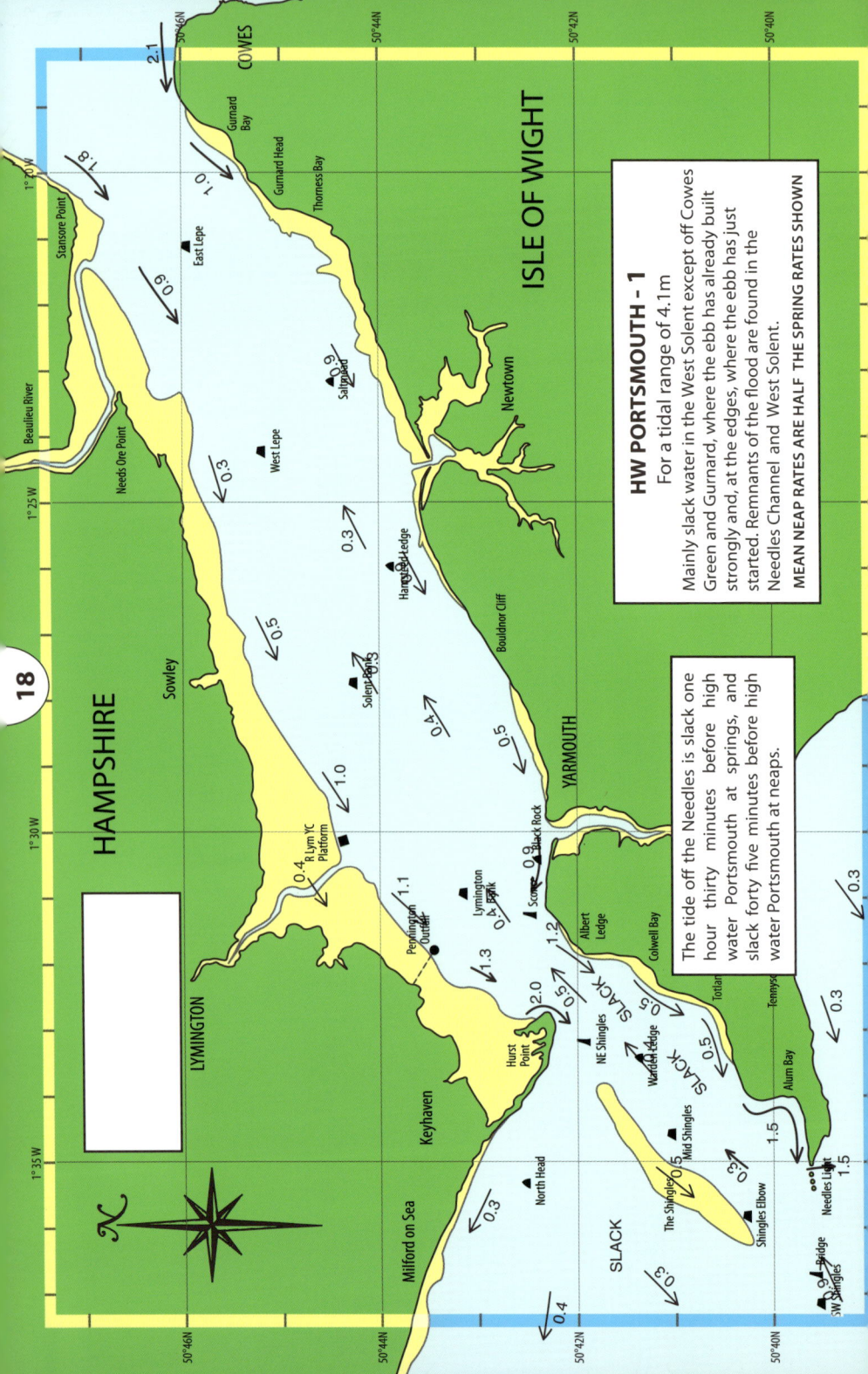

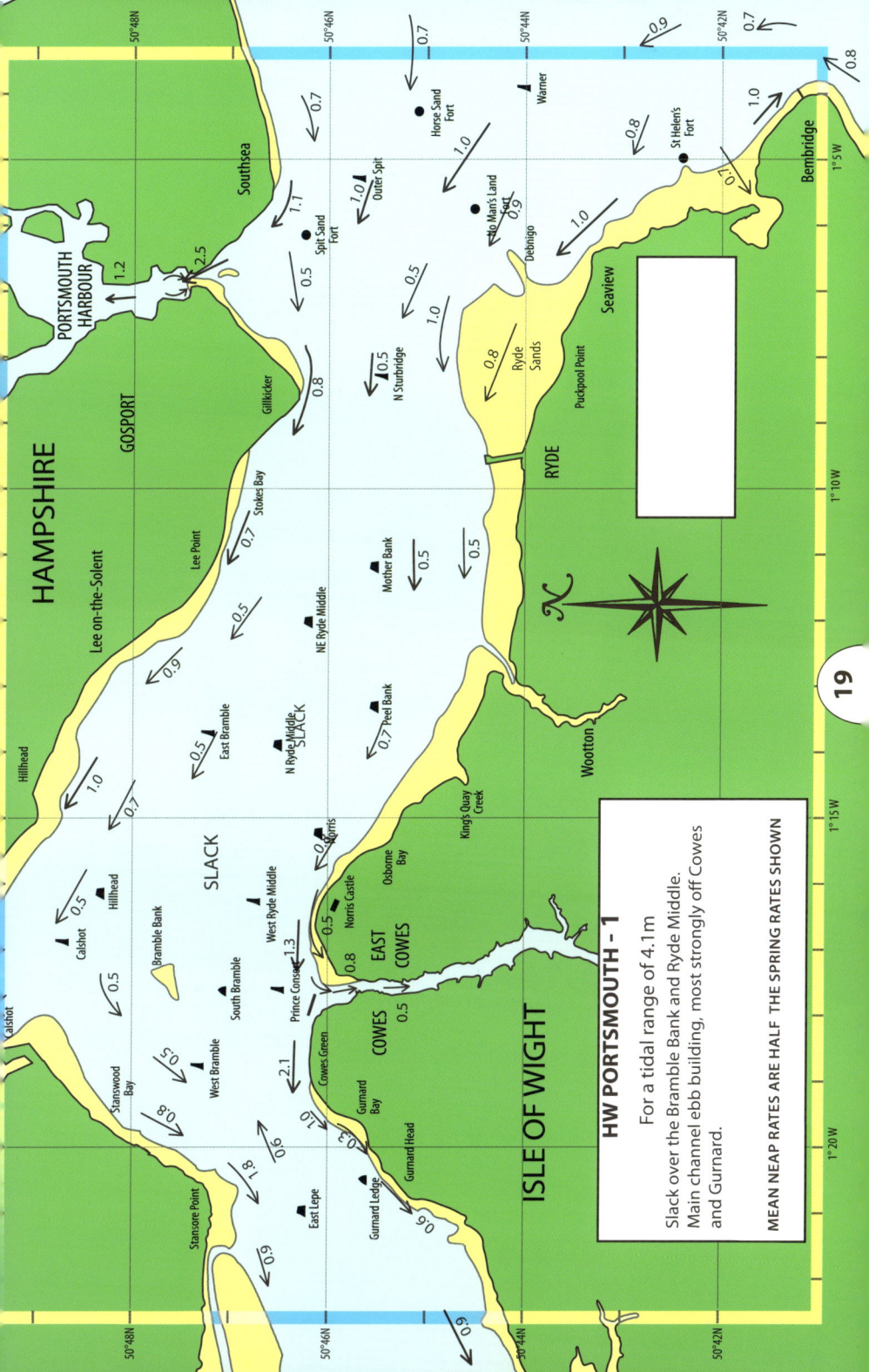

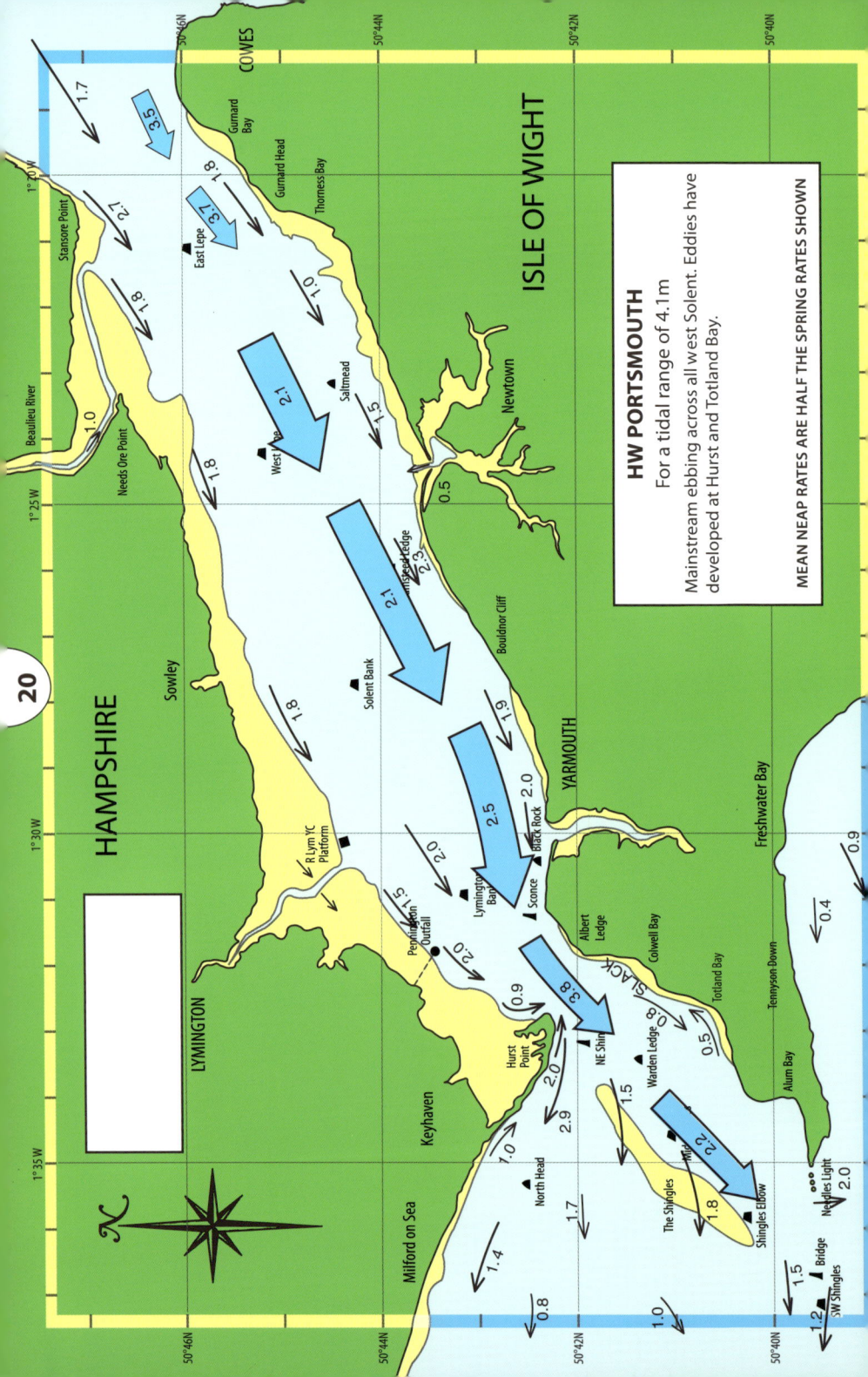

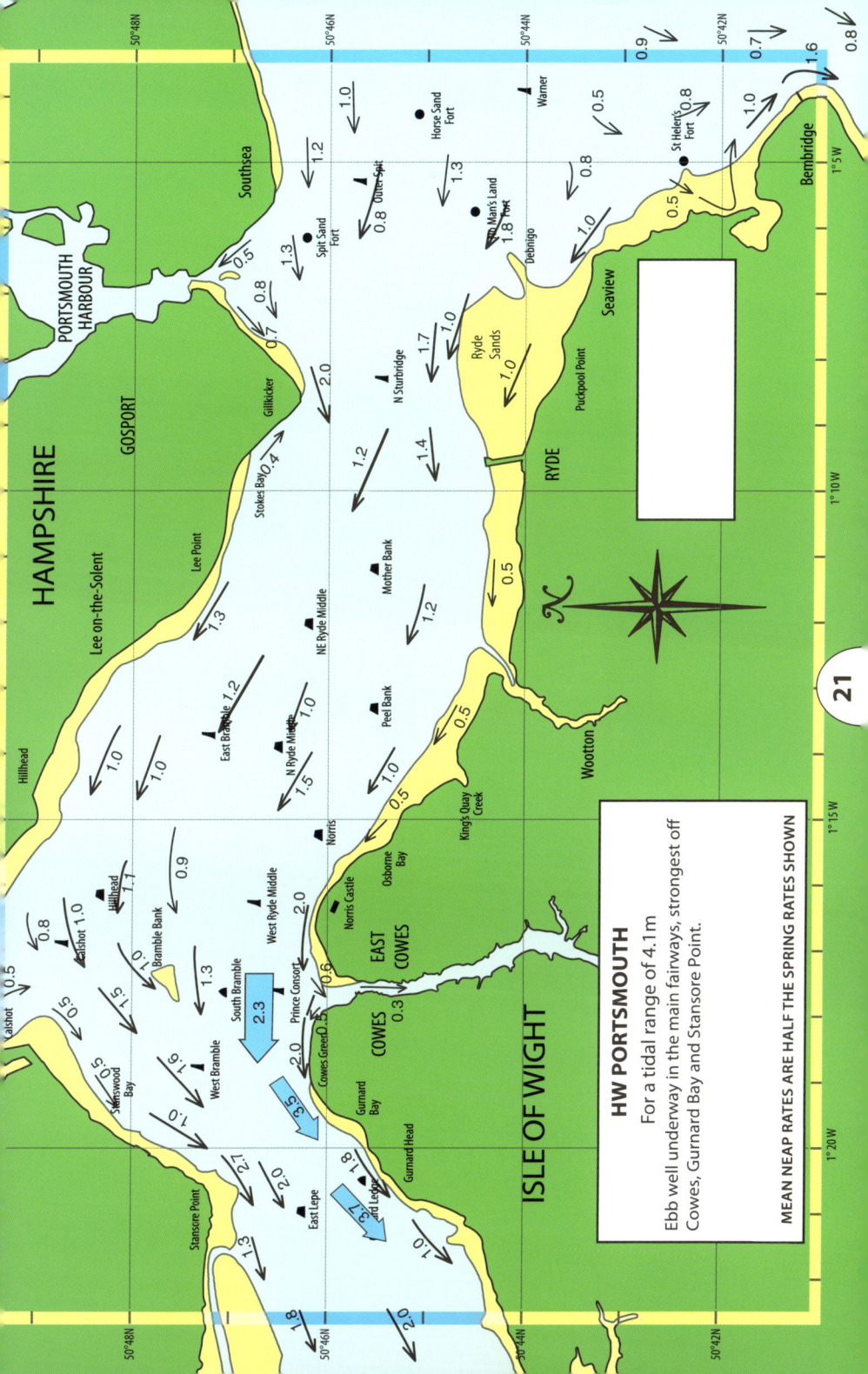

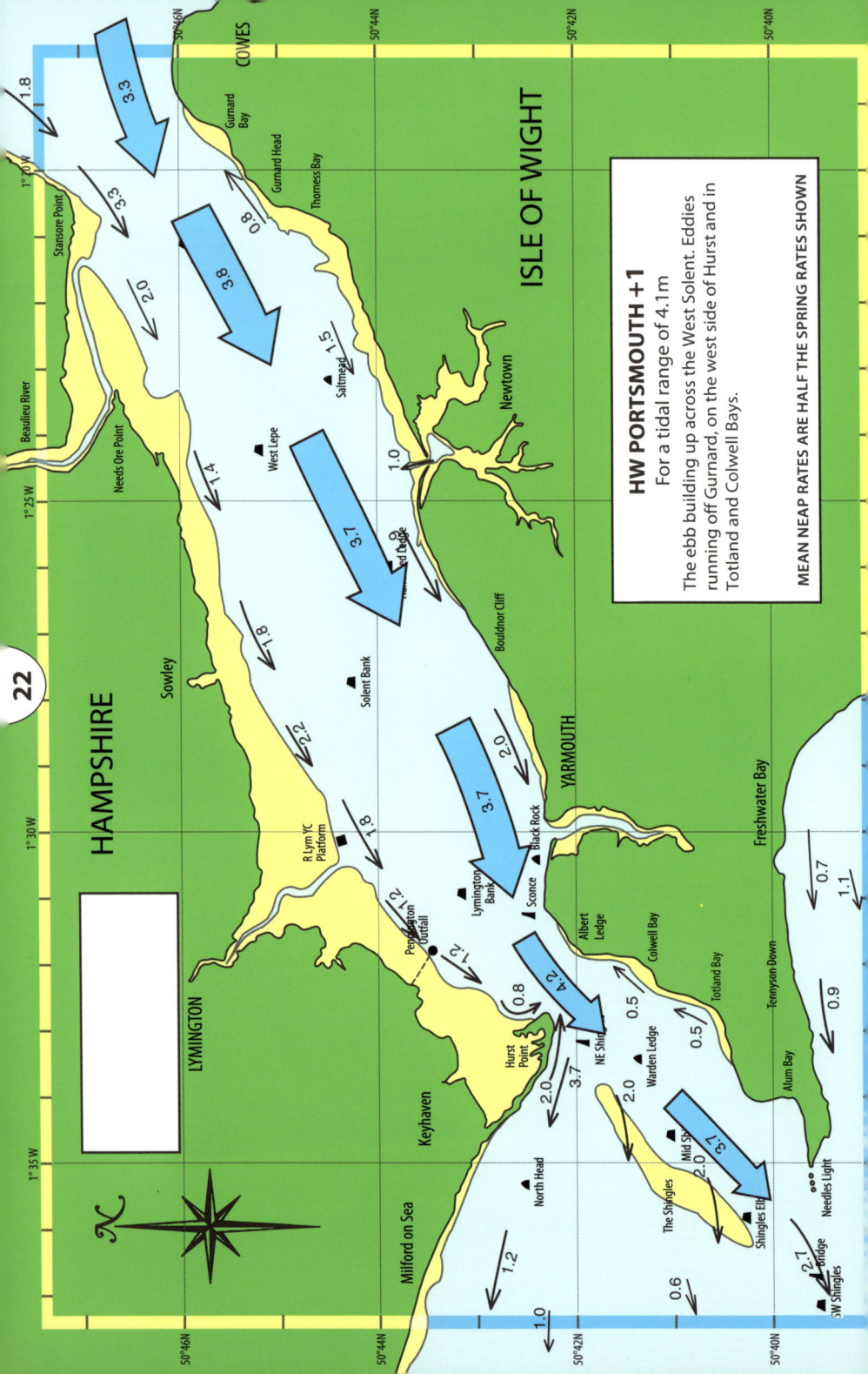

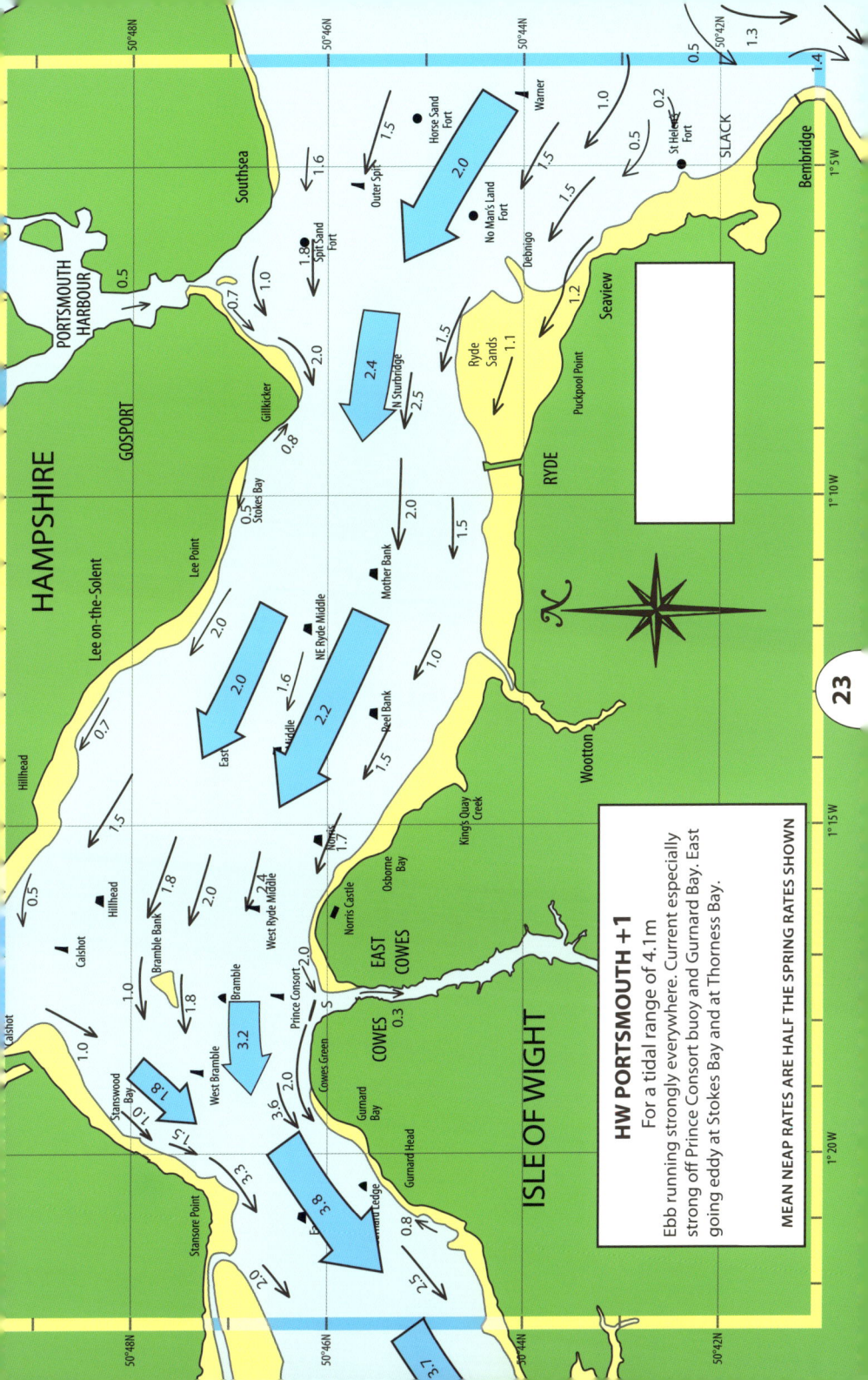

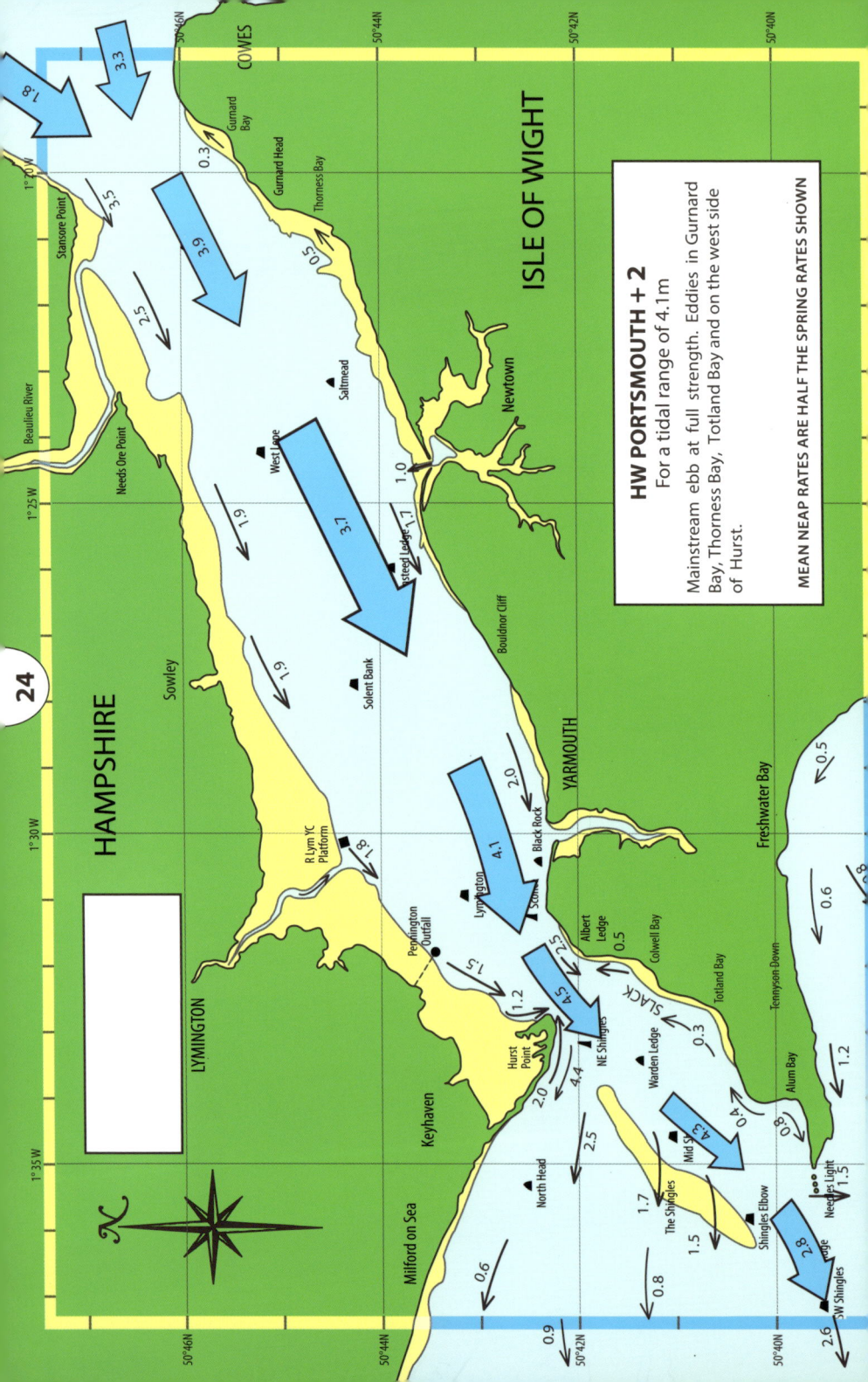

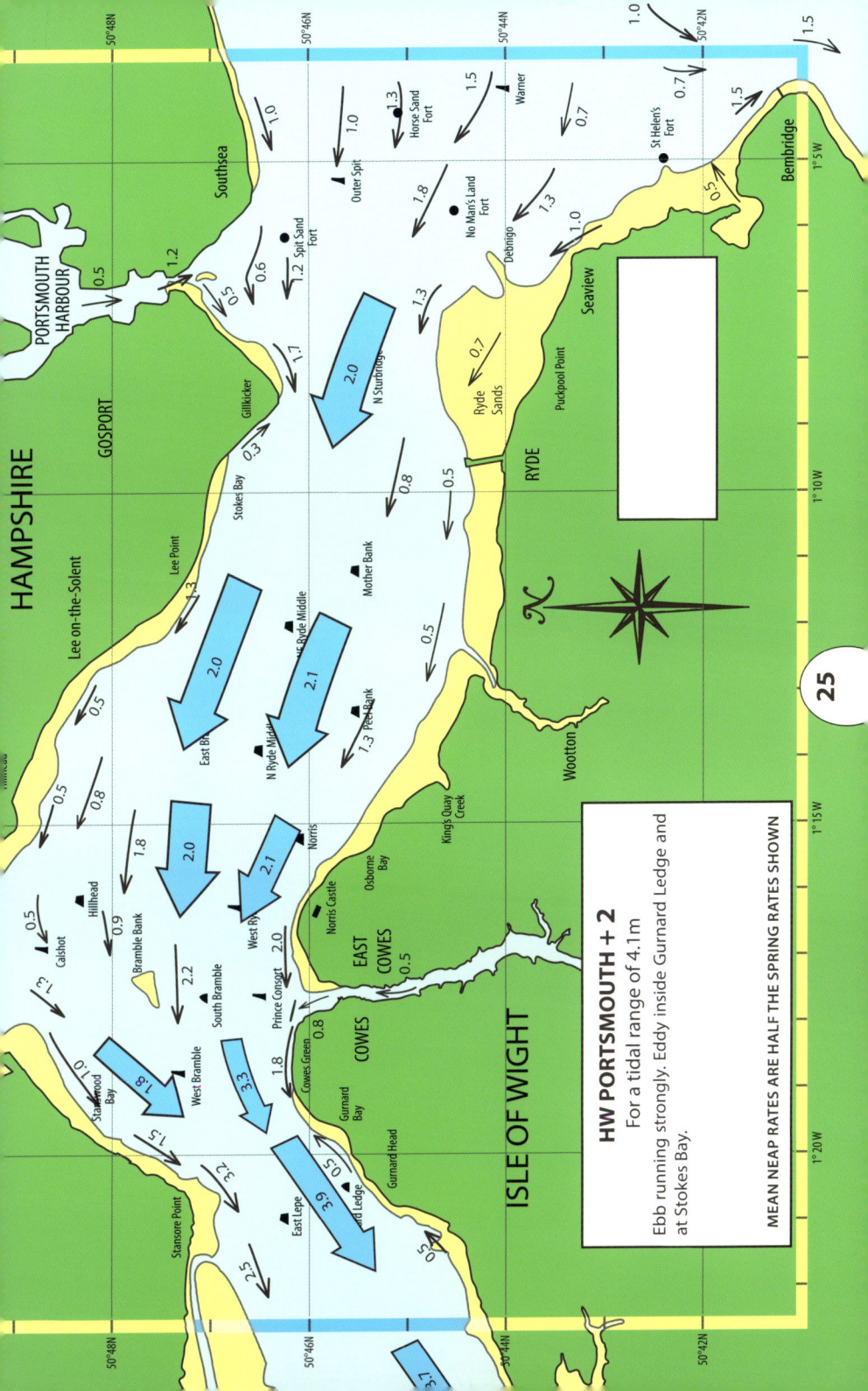

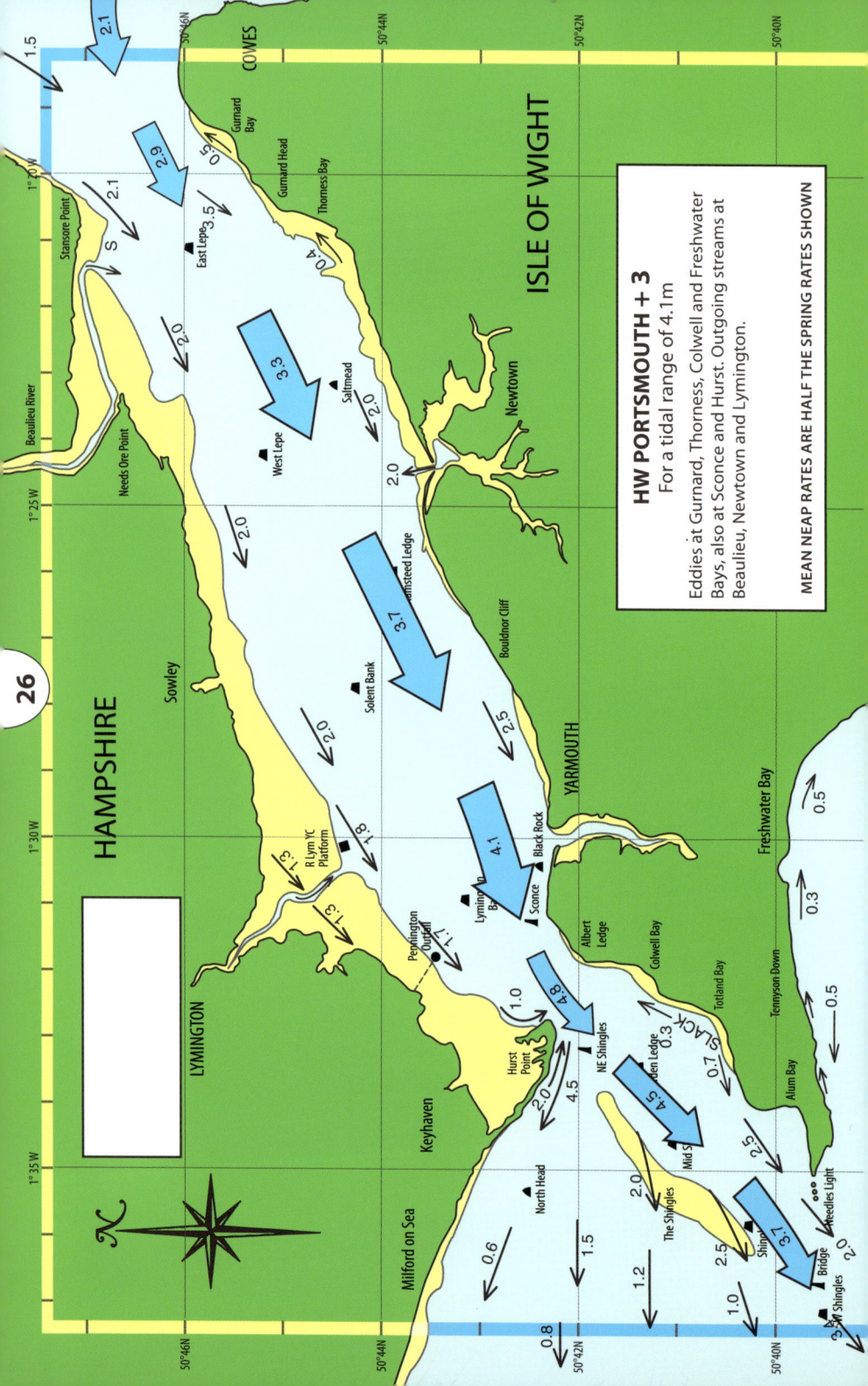

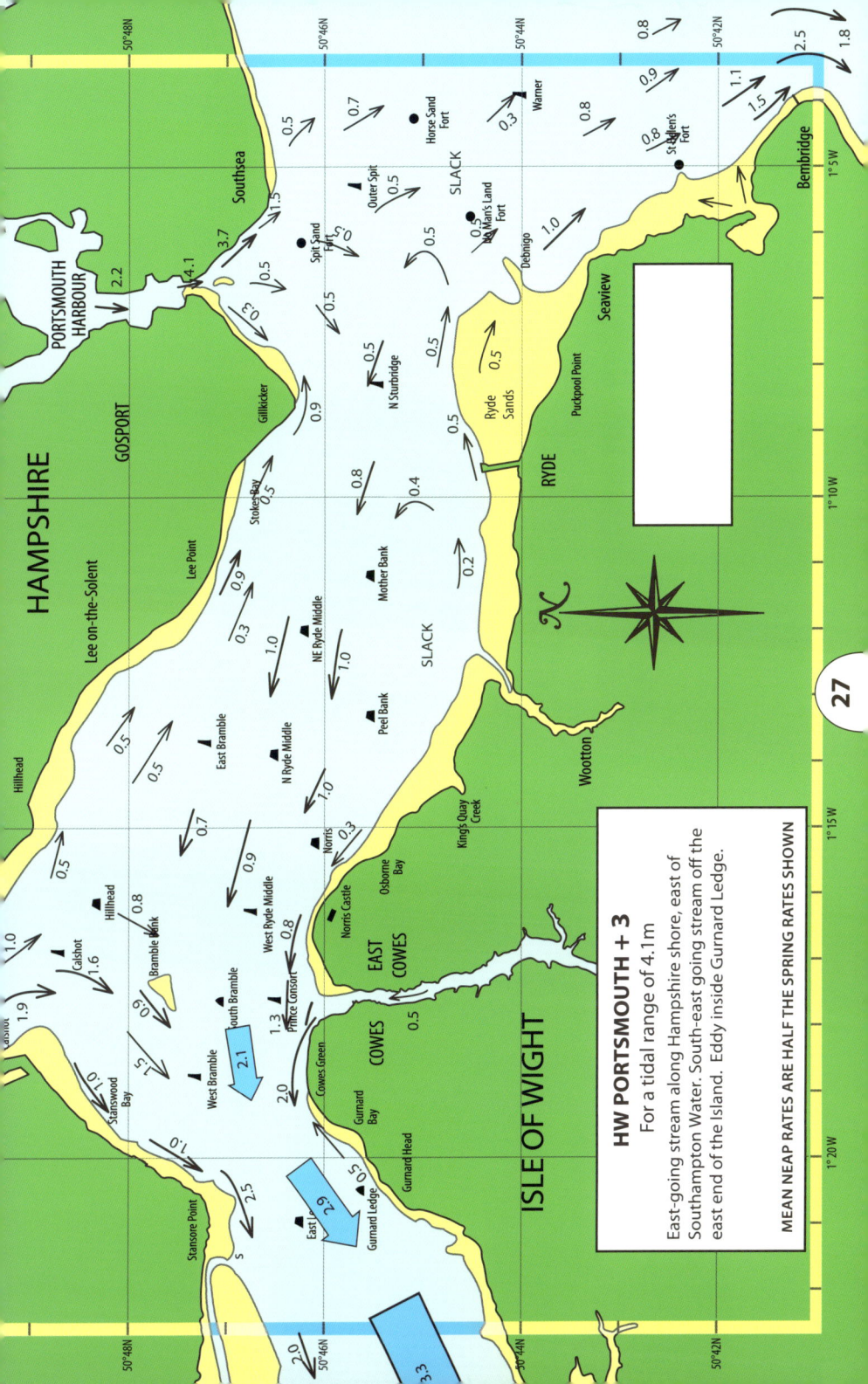

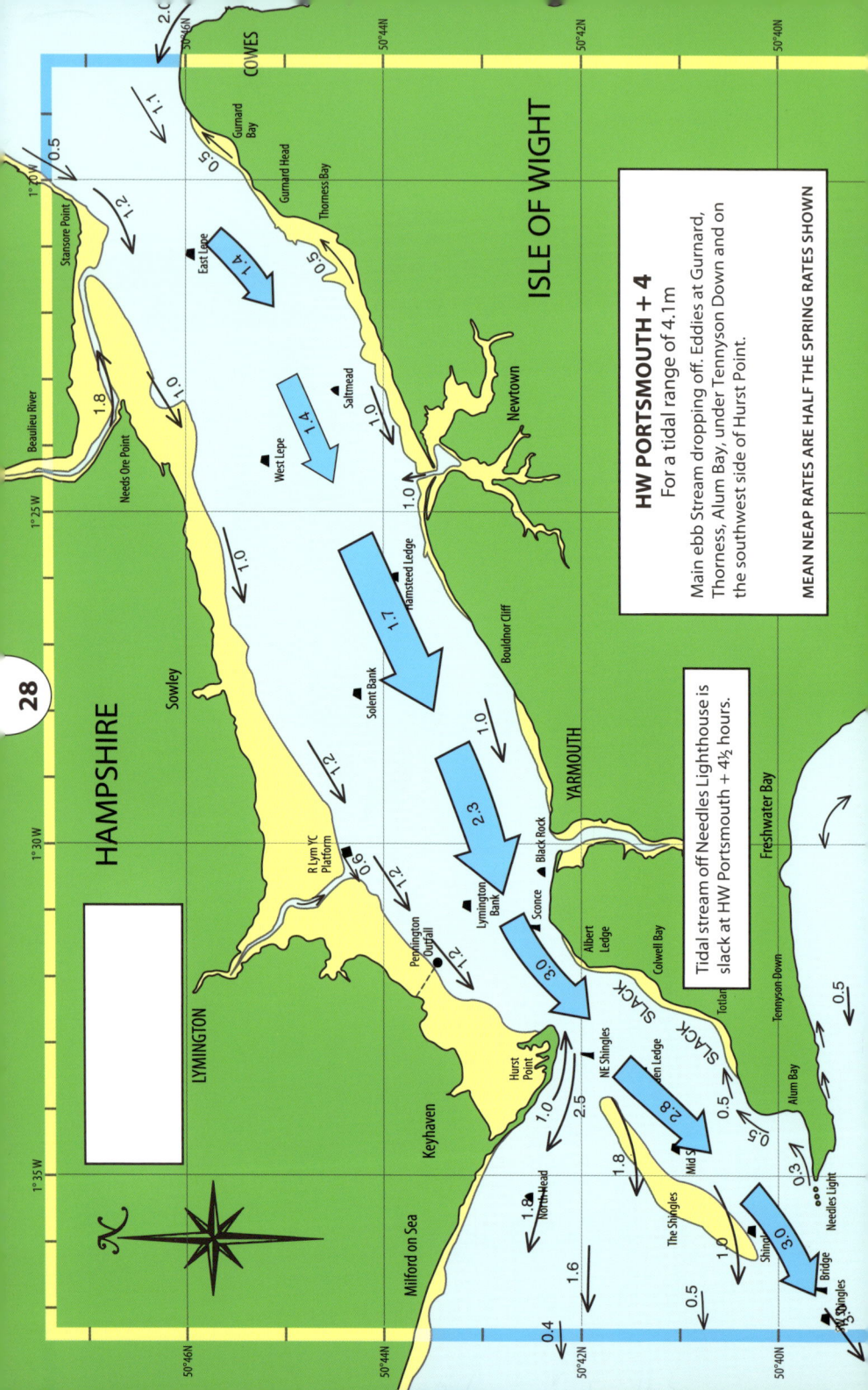

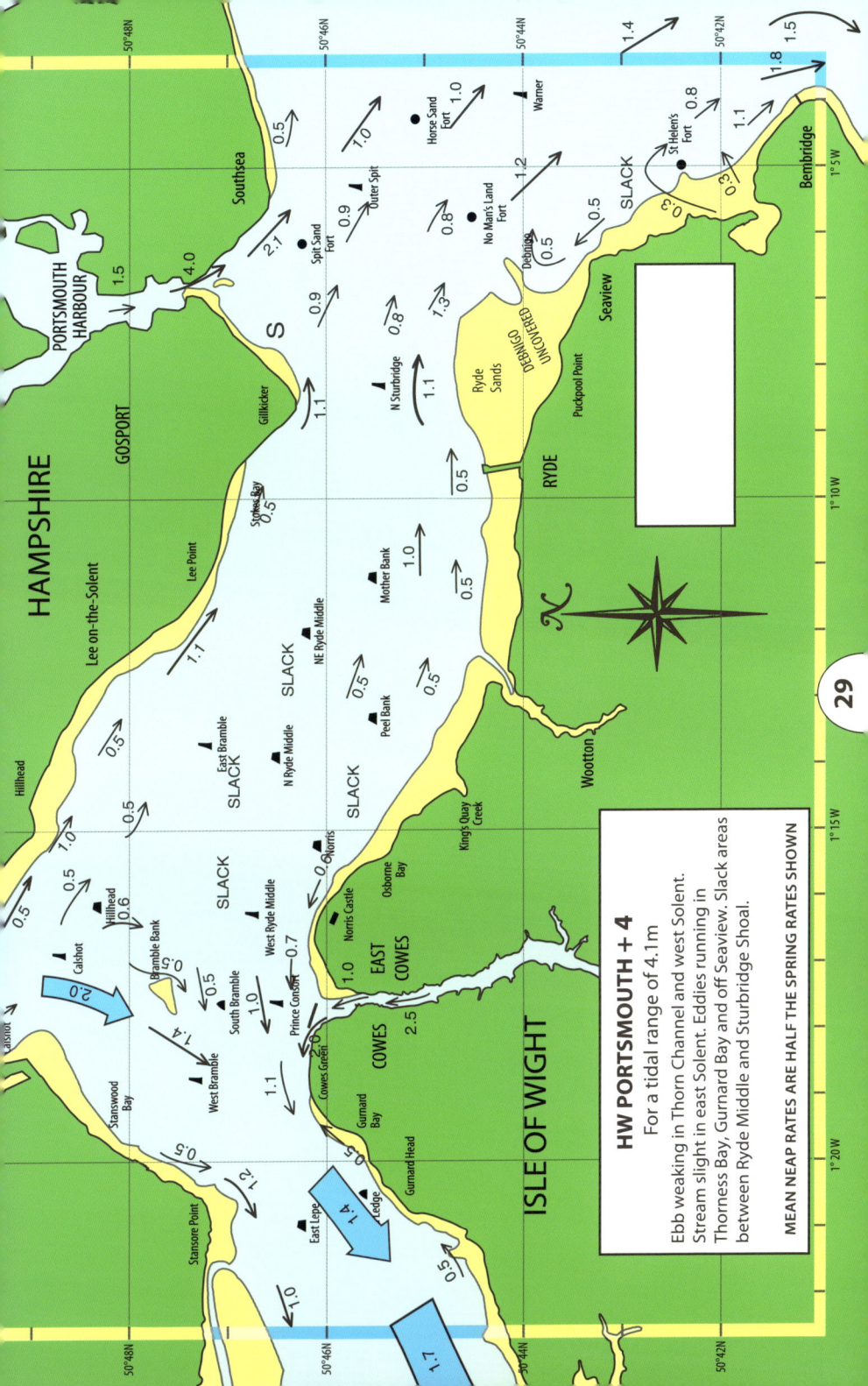

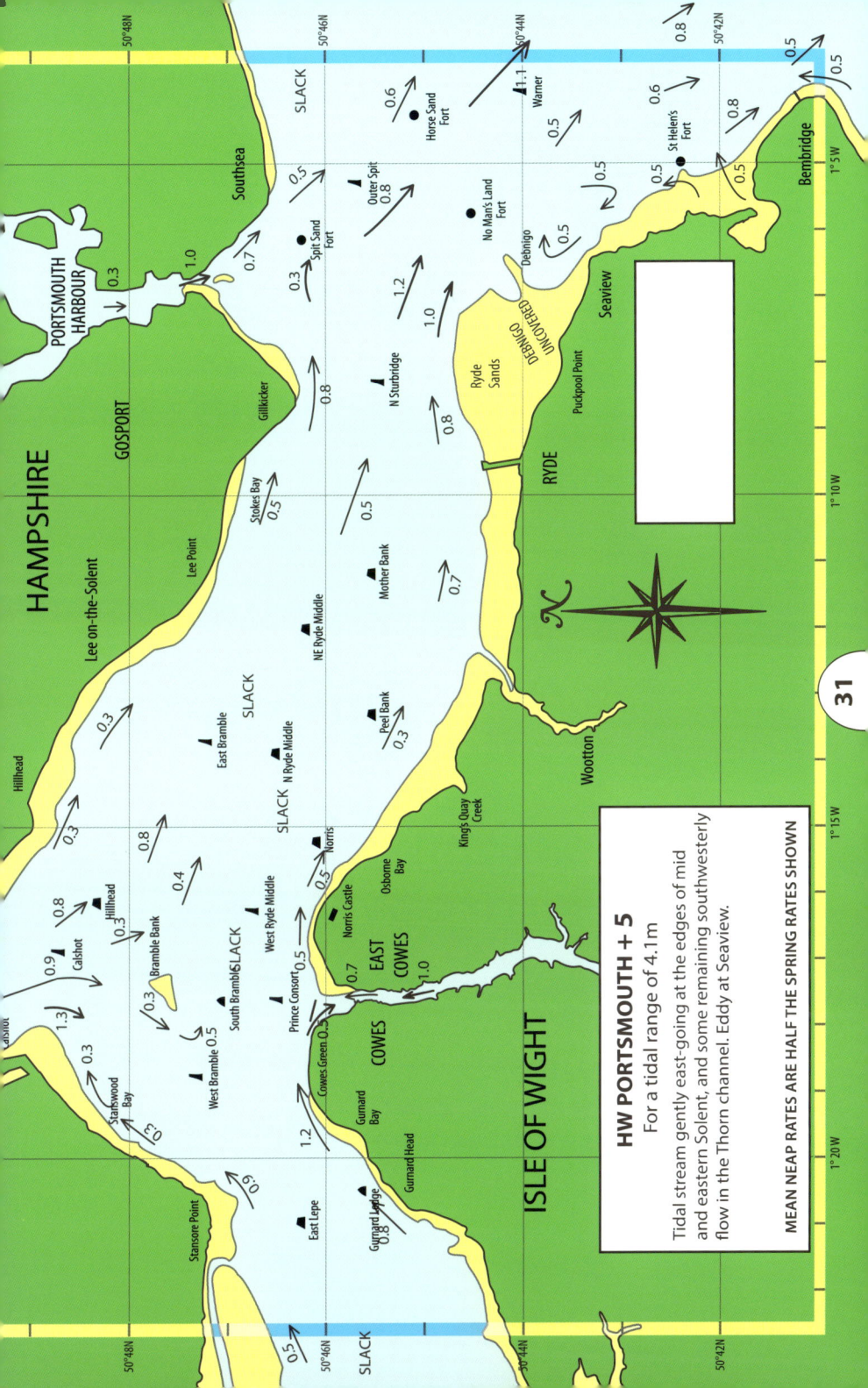

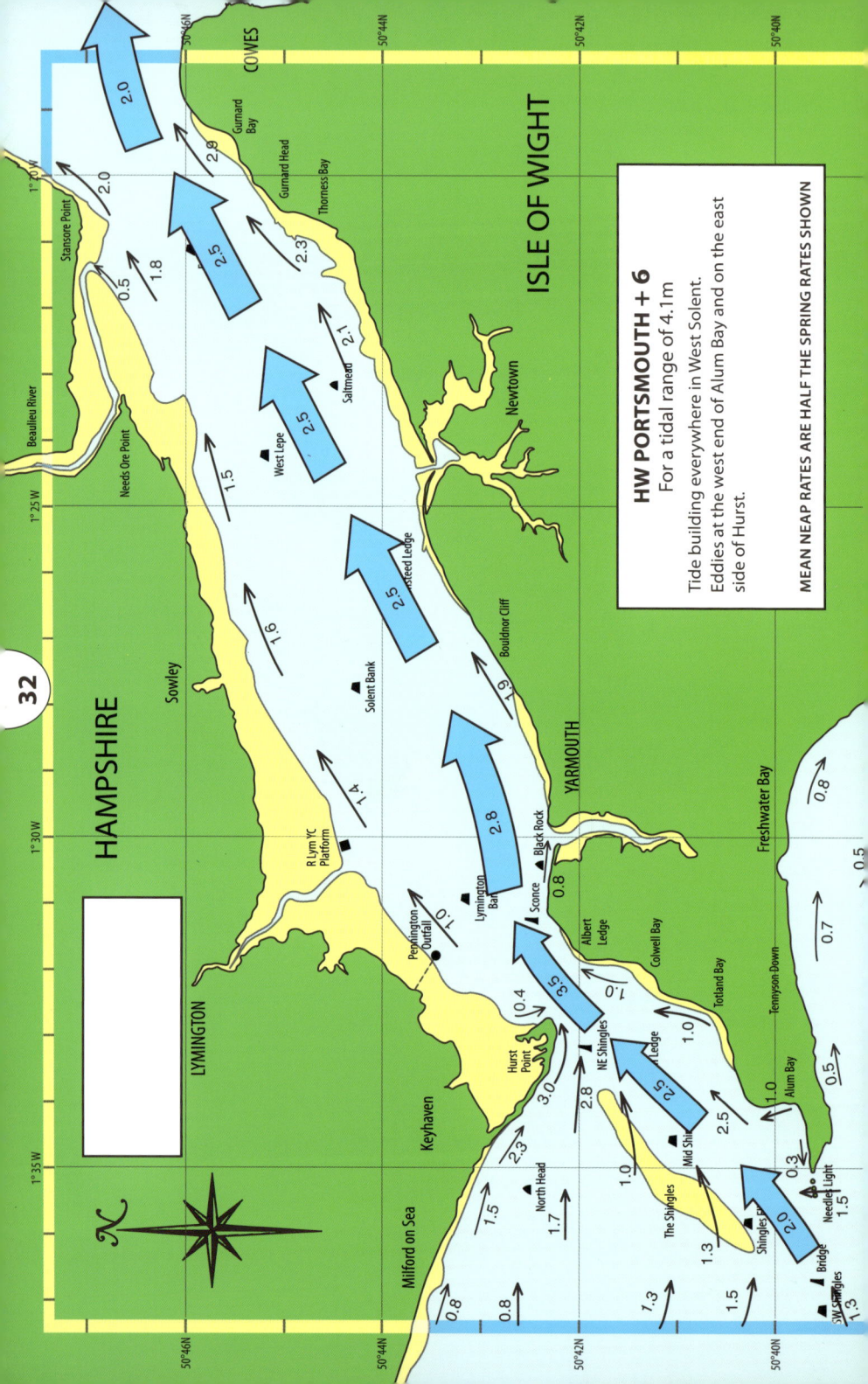

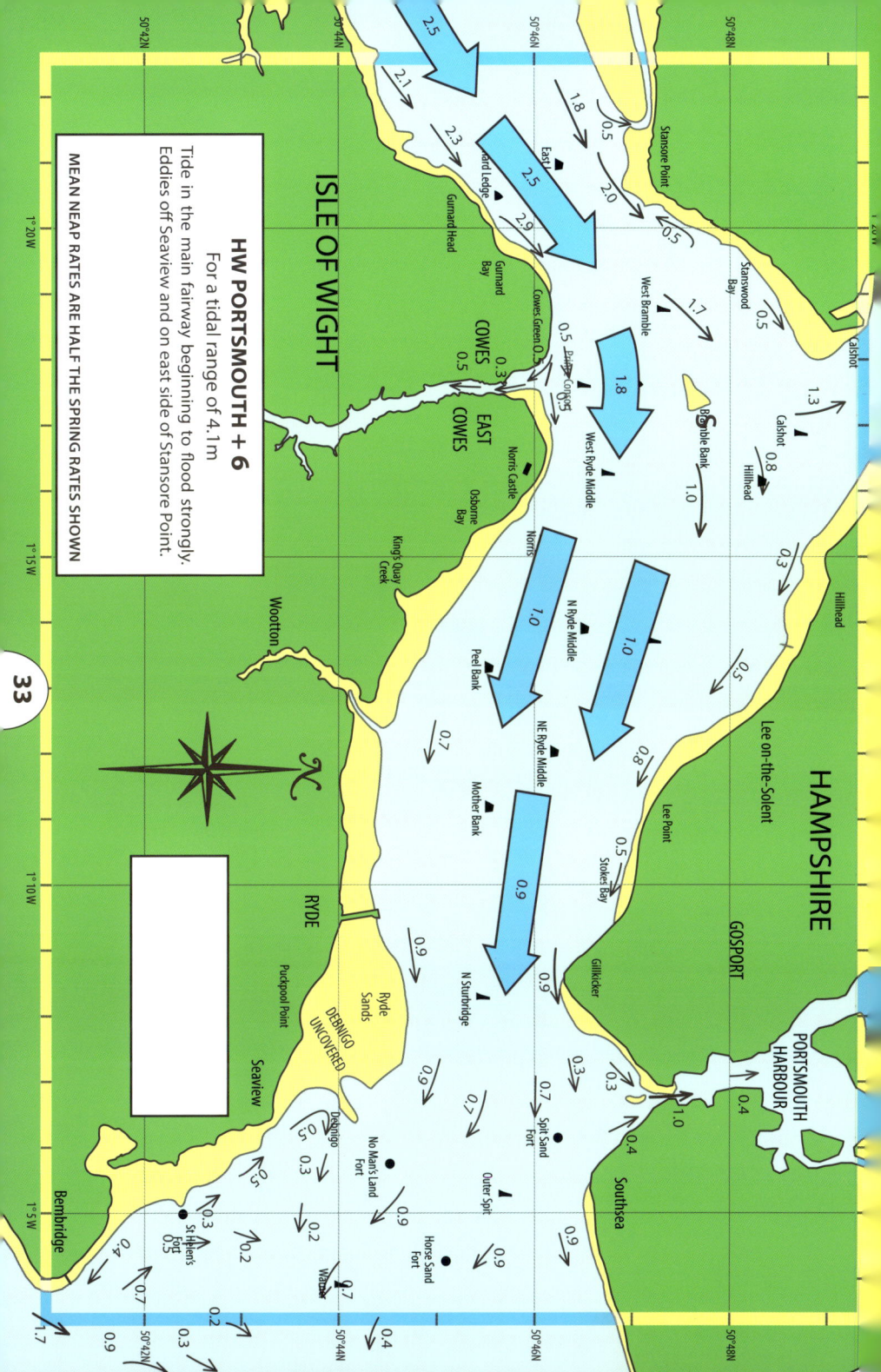

Solent Area Distance Table
(Nautical miles)

From \ To	Chichester Bar	Langstone entrance	Nab Tower	Bembridge entrance	Portsmouth entrance	Wootton entrance	Cowes entrance	Hamble entrance	Southampton (Ocean Village)	Beaulieu entrance	Newtown entrance	Yarmouth entrance	Lymington entrance	Keyhaven entrance	Christchurch entrance
Langstone entrance	3														
Nab Tower	6	7													
Bembridge entrance	7	5	5												
Portsmouth entrance	7	5	10	6											
Wootton entrance	11	8	12	8	5										
Cowes entrance	14	11	15	11	8	4									
Hamble entrance	16	13	18	13	10	8	5								
Southampton (Ocean Village)	20	17	21	19	14	12	9	5							
Beaulieu entrance	17	13	18	13	11	7	3	6	10						
Newtown entrance	20	16	20	16	13	9	8	13	4	3					
Yarmouth entrance	22	20	24	20	16	12	11	16	10	7	2				
Lymington entrance	23	20	24	19	17	13	13	17	8	5	4	2			
Keyhaven entrance	24	22	25	21	18	14	16	21	13	10	6	2	2		
Christchurch entrance	32	29	33	29	22	22	18	25	16	13	11	9	8	6	
Needles Fairway	28	27	31	27	24	20	18	23	14	11	11	7	6	9	6